It's Complicated

-stories from within an ancient conflict-

Kristen McCormack

2012

Dedicated to the peacemakers of our past,
the peacemakers of our present,
and the peacemakers who have yet to become.

"Blessed are the peacemakers, for they will be called children of God."
-Matthew 6:9

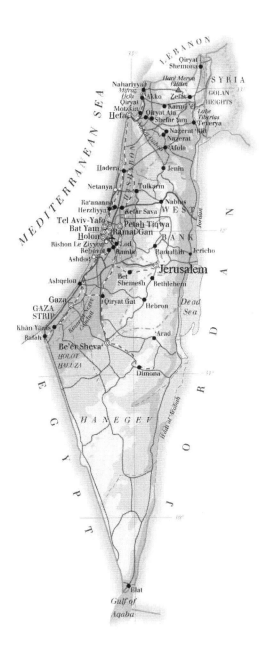

# **Introduction**

I'd like to blame two people for my three decades of not caring
about the history of anything or having any idea about what was
happening in the world that surrounded me. First, I blame my
sister. She was the smart one. I was the sporty one. She loved
books and majored in history. I loved people and played soccer
in college. I played my role, she played hers, and I was content.
Second, I blame my high school history teacher. I had the
unfortunate luck of having her for multiple years, and for all of
those years, even days before graduation, she thought my name
was Sarah. She had a clear dislike for people, teaching, and
history. I had a clear dislike for her, so I never listened, or
learned a thing about history. I'd like to blame two people, but
unfortunately there is only one person that can be held
responsible for my ignorance. Her actual name is Kristen.

Weeks after turning thirty, a close friend invited me to start
caring. He invited me to study and immerse myself in the most
ancient conflict in all the world. He invited me to go to Israel
and the West Bank in order to experience the conflict from
within, in hopes of seeing and hearing each side's truth and
stories. For four months six of my friends and I researched the
current conflict in the state of Israel and the history of the Jewish
and Palestinian people reaching back thousands of years. Once
we were emotionally invested and slightly educated we boarded
a plane and entered into the Holy Land, a land of extraordinary
chaos, a land of complicated injustice, and a land in which the
human beings who occupy it have an undeniable connection and

1

unswerving devotion. And twelve long days later I was more than ready to come home.

I'll give away the end before I even begin. I don't believe there is hope for a solution to the conflict between the Israelis and the Palestinians. I don't believe that we will ever see large-scale and widespread peace in that place. But I do believe there is hope for peace person-by-person, through friendship. And friendship comes when paths collide and stories are shared. Israelis and Palestinians are separated by three-story walls in an effort to isolate and sever all connection. We, on the other hand, have no concrete walls to separate us from the many conflicts and injustices that surround us in our world, yet for the most part we succeed in avoiding them entirely. I no longer have that option, and now I believe it's my responsibility to share what I've learned, and more importantly, what I saw and what I heard. In essence, my desire is to take you there through story so you can see and hear for yourself, and make your own decisions. Here are the stories of the people, including me, entangled in the world's most ancient unholy-holy conflict.

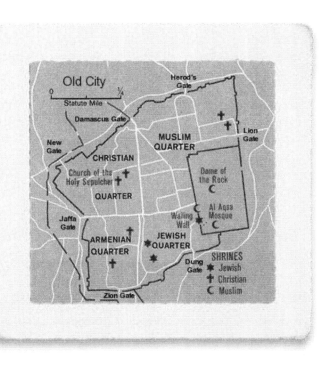

day one

Three movies into our fourteen hour flight to Istanbul, my knees and legs throbbed, and I was jealous. Jealous of the rows and rows of people surrounding me in sleeping-pill induced comas, cuddling their doughnut pillows, and mouths slightly drooping. After a complicated stopover in Turkey and one more flight we reached Tel-Aviv's Ben Gurion Airport early in the morning. By that time my ankles and toes looked like giant baby feet with fat wrinkles and creases. I was thankful for flip flops because the things I had formerly known as my feet were so swollen they would not have fit in shoes.

After making it through Ben Gurion's high security we were met by blazing heat and smiling Issa, our driver. As we pulled out in our air-conditioned, short bus to make the ascension to Jerusalem, Issa took the microphone hanging on his dash and with a "tap tap" to test he began our trip with, "Hello, my name is Issa, and I would like to tell you pieces of my story and take you a different way into the city."

Issa is a Palestinian Christian from Bethlehem. He has a special tourist industry permit which allows him to drive on Israeli roads and through Israeli check points while he is working. Issa drives fast. We were speeding uphill on a new five lane highway.

"The road we are on was just built and is for Israelis and tourists. If you look down to your right at the bottom you will see a dirt road. That is a Palestinian road. Palestinian cars have different plates."

We slowed to a roll as we exited and were waved through a checkpoint guarded by young Israeli soldiers with heavy guns strapped to their bodies. Many parts of the road were lined with barbwire fences or tall concrete walls. We were in the West Bank. When I talked about my trip to friends and family before leaving and mentioned that we would be spending time and staying in the West Bank, often I'd receive a set of widened eyes, and a "Why?"

Issa directed our attention to a large white gate lined with flowers and trimmed bushes off to our right side, not unlike an entrance to a gated neighborhood that we'd see back home in California.

"This is a Jewish Settlement. The Israeli government has control of all of the power and water in the West Bank. They cut off the Palestinian supply as they please. Just a few months ago my family and I were without water for forty-two days straight. We have no water to drink or bathe with, yet they continue to run their sprinklers over the gardens just outside their gates for all to see. This is a very bad problem."

I heard Issa say 'this a is very bad problem' multiple times during our forty-five minute drive into Jerusalem. It reminded me of my last trip to Nepal where the answer to everything was always, "no problem". I knew this trip was not going to be easy before I came. I had read about the injustice on both sides, but it wasn't until I looked out the window and saw part of it, and heard it from a smiling Issa's mouth that the reality and tension of this land began to set into my chest. And then Issa said something that has not wandered far from my thoughts since.

"Jerusalem has been taken, conquered, and changed hands over twenty times throughout the course of history. When the United States speaks about history, you speak in decades. When we speak about history we speak in millennia. You are very young, just a baby of a nation. America is a super power and aspires to control the entire world much like Rome did. What we learn from Jerusalem is today is nothing. Tomorrow, everything could be changed upside down."

As we made our way to our hotel in East Jerusalem, the Muslim side of the city, the streets and sidewalks were flooded with people all walking in the same direction.
"Today is the last Friday of Ramadan. A quarter of a million Muslims will pilgrimage into the Old City today and tomorrow to visit the Al-Aqsa Mosque. Palestinian men over age forty are all given a one-day permit to come into the city. I don't recommend going into the Old City today."

Ramadan is Islam's yearly forty-day fast. Muslims don't eat from sunrise to sunset, and after sunset they feast and party late into the night. In the morning, most sleep in and nothing is open until the afternoon. When the fast is over there is a three-day holiday called Eid ul-Fitr. What we witnessed in East Jerusalem was a three-night party in the streets with loud music and fireworks into the early hours of the morning.

We did not heed Issa's advice to stay clear of the Old City, but instead we dropped our bags at the Capitol Hotel and headed right in with the masses for falafel. We walked down the chaotic and crawling main street alongside the outer wall of the city until we reached the Damascus Gate and entered into the Old City. For the most part there are no cars within the walls, the narrow pathways of the Muslim Quarter are lined with market-style shops and paved in slippery limestone. Many of the reed-thin streets give the feeling of walking through an echoey, damp tunnel, with only bits and pieces of light breaking in through the gaps between overhangs and laundry lines connecting the old buildings leaning in overhead.

It doesn't take long to notice that Palestinian boys and girls run the streets with toy guns, shooting and pointing them at whoever steps into range. I prefer the orange to the black. I came to

Israel knowing that the everywhere-presence of guns would be hard for me. A few years ago while traveling, a friend and I were attacked by thieves, guns to our heads. I will never stop traveling, but the way I see life as I travel is different now. Fear does not run me; I choose to give people who don't look like me the benefit of the doubt, but the sight of a gun will always steal my breath and make my heart pound. IDF Israeli soldiers have a quiet presence in most places, standing in twos and threes watching. Their heavy guns, M-4s and M-16s, aren't as unnerving as I had assumed. More than anything, they made me feel safe. I think it is because I knew that every Israeli boy and girl has to join the IDF, Israeli Defense Force, for two years, straight out of high school. What I was seeing that first day weren't angry, power-hungry people holding big guns. I was seeing teenagers with nice haircuts sweat in the unbearable heat, under thick uniforms, bullet proof vests, and heavy equipment.

My favorite thing to do while traveling is to eat. We sat down at tables hiding from the sun under umbrellas and ordered falafel sandwiches. Falafel, an Arab staple, are deep fried balls of ground-up chickpeas and fava beans, with pickled vegetables, smothered in tahini sauce and wrapped in the fluffiest, most amazing pita you'll ever taste. I actually ordered a shawarma sandwich, similar, but instead of falafel balls you get meat. The meat is a light brown mystery mix of lamb, turkey, beef, chicken, or goat shaved off a rotating spit. With full stomachs we continued on through the Old City to find Hezekiah's Tunnel.

In 701 BC, a few centuries shy of three thousand years ago, King Hezekiah had a special tunnel chipped out of the rock that led under the City of David, currently beneath where we were walking, in order to re-route the Gihon Spring. Hezekiah did this to ensure water to his people within the safety of his walled city during a feared attack by the Assyrians. He was right to be afraid because twenty years later, the Assyrians conquered his city. He had two groups of men chip out his tunnel with hammers and pick-axes, bucket-brigade style. They began from either end, about a third of a mile apart, and dug toward each other on a slant in order to meet in the middle years later.

We paid 17 shekels, about four to a dollar, for a ticket to walk a very old, dark, and wet tunnel. The tunnel is no different than it was 2,700 years ago. There are no hand rails, lights, or "watch your head" signs. But there is very cold water running over your feet and sometimes it's as deep as your waist. I had no light, going around tight bends, I'd lose the light coming from my friend's phone behind me, so I'd hold my breath and use my hands to feel the way. This is not a tunnel for big people, the claustrophobic, or those afraid of the dark. I spent most of it ducking, at 5'6" I don't duck often, and for the majority of the tunnel there were only inches between my shoulders and the rough carved sides of the rock. In America we'd never be allowed to do this, the risk is far too great, and surely it would all be behind glass. We'd only been in this place for a handful of hours and it was already very clear that whoever has control of the water has control of the people.

Coming out of the tunnel and into the harsh afternoon light outside the city walls, we were surrounded by excavations. Recently, during a sewage piping project, they found remains of the City of David. The area, part of the Palestinian village of Silwan, was deemed a Jewish archaeological site, and the land in question has been confiscated for excavations. Not far from where we were standing we could see the fresh dirt where thirty-five Palestinian houses had been bulldozed and demolished. Because the City of David surrounds Hezekiah's Tunnel, within the Muslim Quarter, the Israelis have taken over the tunnel and the area around it. This means not long ago our shekels would have gone to the Muslims who made their living from tourism and the shops that surround the tunnel, but our shekels went towards funding the excavations and demolitions. It was a very long walk back to East Jerusalem.

Al-Aqsa Mosque built	709 AD
Dome of the Rock built on Temple Mount	691 AD
Islam Army under Uma takes Jerusalem	637 AD
Muhammad's Night Journey	621 AD
Islam begins	600 AD
Helena built Holy Sepulchre	300 AD
Romans destroy Second Temple	70 AD
Christianity begins	30 AD
Herod renovates Temple/builds Western Wall	20 BC
Roman Empire conquer Jerusalem	63 BC
Hasmoneans (Jewish Maccabees) take Jerusalem	141 BC
Second Temple built under Persian rule	551 BC
Temple destroyed by the Babylonians	586 BC
Solomon's Temple built	900 BC
David takes Jerusalem/City of David	1000 BC
Jerusalem is a Canaanite city	1500 BC
Abraham/Isaac sacrifice on Mount Moriah	2200 BC

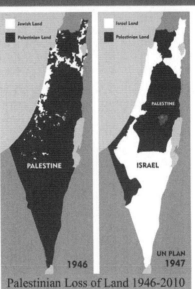

Palestinian Loss of Land 1946-2010

The History of Jerusalem

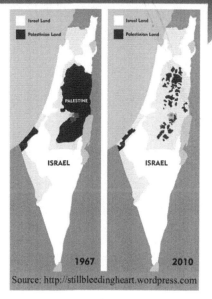

Turks take Jerusalem	1076 AD
Crusaders take Jerusalem for the Christians	1099 AD
Saladin takes Jerusalem for the Muslims	1187 AD
Ottoman Empire takes Jerusalem	1516 AD
WWI/British take Jerusalem under mandate	1917 AD
Six-Day War/Israel takes Jerusalem	1967 AD
War of Independence/Jordan takes Jerusalem	1948 AD
First Intifada	1987 AD
Failed Oslo Accord peace talks	1993 AD
Second Intifada	2000 AD
Barrier wall constructed	2005 AD
Present	

Israel Land
Palestinian Land

PALESTINE

ISRAEL

1967

Israel Land
Palestinian Land

ISRAEL

2010

11

day two

In the morning my roommate and I made our way down to the hotel's dining room to meet the rest of our group for breakfast. The spread of vegetables, hummus, boiled eggs, homemade bologna and bread was impressive. This would be the day we'd see the Jewish, Muslim, and Christian holy sites in and around the Old City. We would also walk the circumference of the Old City for a birds-eye view via the top of the wall that encircles it. Our day would be on foot. The entire state of Israel is said to be the size of Rhode Island. Rhode Island is so small its name never even fits in its state. In my mind all the places I've read about in the Bible have always been so much bigger than what I was seeing. Jon, who had been to Israel quite a few times, told us, "This whole thing is like Monopoly. You've been collecting the pieces and the cards your whole life, and today you get to walk on the board. Things are going to start making a new kind of sense."

Another sixteen shekels and we all had tickets to do the Rampart's Walk. Rampart is defined as a defensive wall. Not far from the Jaffa gate we climbed up double-thick and slightly uneven stairs to the top of the fortified wall that encloses the city into just over one-third of a square mile. The wall stretches for almost three miles, with an average thickness of ten feet, and reaches to as high as 49 feet. The wall we were walking on was built by a Sultan in 1537 AD during the Ottoman Rule. The walls of the Old City are much like an accordion in the way they have continually contracted and expanded over the millennia,

13

depending on who knocked them down and who later rebuilt them. Jerusalem is one of the world's oldest cities, and in her existence she has been attacked 52 times, besieged 23 times, captured and recaptured 44 times, and completely destroyed twice. The name Jerusalem, or *Orshalim* from Hebrew origins, comes from the Canaanites who first built a temple on Mount Moriah to worship their god, Shalom, the god of peace. From its roots the name Jerusalem means city of peace. If only the Canaanites could see their 'City of Peace' now.

Mount Moriah, a modest hill in the center of everything, is a strange spot that seems to have more historical happenings and spiritual connections to three different groups of people than any other spot on the planet. In order to have any chance at understanding what is happening on the ground today in Israel we need to look at the roots. And the roots are over 3,000 years deep. In high school I would have skimmed this next section and missed the point. But I recently learned that history is fascinating, and connects all things. The more you know, the more the world starts to make sense. The more you know about yesterday, the more you understand today.

A good place to start is from the beginning. According to Jewish tradition God scooped up dust from Mount Moriah to form Adam, the world's first human being. Then we jump to Abraham in 2200 BC. Abraham is considered the founding patriarch, or father, of the world's largest religions, Judaism, Christianity, and Islam. Abraham's job from God was to be the father of all nations, but his wife Sarah was infertile. You can't be the father of all nations if you don't have any sons. In a panic move, Sarah convinced Abraham to sleep with their Egyptian servant, Hagar, to produce an heir, Ishmael. But fourteen years later, Sarah got pregnant, with Isaac, who would become Ishmael's younger brother from another mother. About a year later, Ishmael and his mother were no longer needed and sent away angry with no inheritance or real claim to the family. But Ishmael was still made into a great nation. He had twelve sons who became the chiefs of Arab tribes like the Egyptians, the Assyrians, the Babylonians, and the Persians. According to Islamic tradition, the prophet Mohammad, who founded Islam, ascended from Ishmael. Back in Canaan we have Abraham, Sarah, and Isaac living as a family excited to fulfill their

14

promise. And then God told Abraham to go up to the top of Mount Moriah and sacrifice Isaac. I imagine Abraham was quite confused. God wanted him to climb a mountain, bring a bunch of wood, kill his only, very important to the future of the entire world, son, and then set him on fire. But he did it. Well, he almost did it. God stopped him at the last second. It almost sounds like a very sick joke, much like the name Jerusalem meaning 'City of Peace."

Isaac stayed in Canaan, and through him and his son Jacob we have the twelve tribes of Israel. God changed Jacob's name to Israel, at that time Israel wasn't a place it was a person. The descendants of Israel, formally known as Jacob, are the Israelites. Through Isaac is the bloodline of the Jews, and later the Christians, and through Ishmael is the bloodline of the Muslims.

We have a long way to go. The Egyptian Pharaohs were the first to conquer the land around 1800 BC. The Israelites were exiled to become slaves in Egypt until Moses brought them back to their 'Promised Land' in 1450 BC. Jump ahead 450 years, and King David, of Isaac's blood, conquered the Jebusites of Jerusalem, and built the City of David. The City of David is what is currently being dug up around Hezekiah's tunnel. King David was succeeded by his son, Solomon, who built the Jewish Temple on top of the center of everything, Mount Moriah. 180 years later the Assyrians, of Ishmael's blood, took the City of David despite King Hezekiah's ingenious attempt at supplying his people with water in order to ever-defend his city from inside its ramparts. Eventually, the Babylonians, again of Ishmael's blood, conquered the City of Peace, exiled the Jewish people to be slaves in Babylon, and destroyed the Temple.

Thirty-five years later, in 551 BC, Persia conquered the Babylonians, and in an effort to stay in charge for a while, they invited the Jews back into the city and allowed them to rebuild a second temple. But the Jews weren't in control of the city again until 164 BC, when a Jewish rebel army, the Maccabees, revolted against the reigning Syrians who were under Alexander the Great's influence. The Greek influence of the time was of the "cosmopolitan" idea that all should be "world citizens". The Jews were being pressured and forced to lose their religion, some even had circumcisions surgically reversed. In light of that and the temple being desecrated the Maccabees revolted and won. And in a partnership with the Hasmoneans they ruled for almost one hundred years, free to be as Jewish as they wanted, until the Romans conquered in 63 BC.

With the Romans came Herod. He was an over-the-top, mentally-ill king who had more riches than he could spend, and an obsessive affection for big things. He made massive expansions and additions to the Jewish Temple, including building what is now called the Western Wall, or Wailing Wall. At the turn of the next century Jesus enters the Holy City still under Roman rule, and Christianity is introduced. He was forced to carry his own cross as he walked through the city on Via Dolorosa to his death just outside the walls on a small hill called Golgotha.

In 66 AD, the Jewish Zealots revolted against Rome. For several years they waged war with Rome and in 70 AD they lost. Rome destroyed their beloved second temple, and they were exiled from the city once again. At the end of the Roman period, Emperor Constantine converted to Christianity and in 313 AD legalized Christianity, making it the official religion of the Roman Empire. This would have been quite a stir considering that in ancient Rome they were known for feeding the Christians to lions for entertainment. When Constantine's mother, Helena, came to Jerusalem for a visit, she decided to erect a few holy sites for Jesus and had a new pagan temple, that was built on Mount Moriah, destroyed. In 335 AD, Helena had the Holy Sepulchre built in what is now the Christian quarter of the Old City. The Holy Sepulchre is a massive church topped with a decadent dome, marking the spot where Jesus was hung on the cross and holding the tomb Jesus

was said to have been buried in and risen from. That spot, known as Golgotha, was now within the walls because the city expanded and the walls had been moved out. During this time, Christians were allowed to live and worship freely within the city, yet Jews were still banned from even entering the city, with the exception of one day a year to visit the Western Wall.

Over 200 years later, the prophet Muhammad is born in Mecca, Saudi Arabia, of Ishmael's blood. According to Islamic tradition, when he was forty years old, the angel Gabriel revealed to him the Quran, and from there we have the birth of Islam. When Muhammad was fifty-one, in 621 AD, the angel Gabriel came back to him and instructed him to get on a white donkey with wings that had sprouted from its thighs. He then flew on his donkey from Mecca to Mount Moriah and landed on the exposed rock where Abraham attempted Isaac's Sacrifice, and where the Holy of Holies within the temple was formerly located. From there he was met by Abraham, Moses, and Jesus, before he ascended up to heaven by way of a golden ladder, or rope, or maybe silver steps. According to one of the mom of a Muslim student of mine, Muhammad ascended with no ladder, rope, or steps. When I talked to her husband, he did some checking and assured me it was actually steps of gold and silver. However it was that he got up there, when he did, Allah gave him a message and he came back down and flew back to Mecca.

Sixteen years after "Muhammad's Night Journey", in 637 AD, an Islamic Army under Caliph Umar conquered Jerusalem. Under Umar's rule, Jews were made to wear a yellow patch on their sleeve, and no Jew or Christian was allowed to live within the city. Perhaps to assert the supremacy of Islam, the impressive Dome of the Rock was built in 691 AD on the foundation of the Temple Mount, over the sacred rocks that represent three major pieces of religious history. The Dome of the Rock was built just a little bigger than the Holy Sepulchre, and is quite possibly the most photographed building in all of the world. Its gold dome reflects the sun and because it sits at the highest point in the center of the city, it can be clearly seen from almost anywhere in the surrounding area. Eighteen years later, the Muslims built the Al-Aqsa Mosque across from the Dome of the Rock at the south end of the Temple Mount. Al-Aqsa means 'from afar' because of the three main holy sites for the Muslims, Mecca, Medina, and Jerusalem, it is the farthest from Mecca. This is the site that a quarter of a million Muslims pilgrimage to for prayer at Ramadan's end.

In 1076 AD, the Turks captured Jerusalem, persecuted the Christians, and closed down all Christian holy sites. Upon receiving a letter informing of the terrible situation the Christians were facing in Jerusalem, the Pope was enraged. In France, Pope Urban II gave a speech from a high scaffold (he must have been yelling) exhorting his people to wage war against the Muslims and restore the Christians to their rightful place in the Holy City. His words were, "Christians, hasten to help your brothers in the East, for they are being attacked. Arm for the rescue of Jerusalem under your captain Christ. Wear his cross as your badge. If you are killed your sins will be pardoned."

The zealous volunteers sewed red crosses to their sleeves and walked their way from France to Turkey in the name of Jesus. Apparently, they had no real leader and killed a lot of Jews along the way. Perhaps the Pope preferred to support his war with prayer from afar. When they entered Turkey, the Crusaders were 10,000 strong, and from there they marched on to the Holy City. Blood everywhere, they killed everyone, all 70,000 human beings within the walls, for Jesus. They made the Dome of the Rock into a church, even climbed to the top and put a cross up there for all to see. The Al-Aqsa mosque became a palace for the knights and a stable for their horses.

It's about here in this story that I want to throw up. If Sarah would have just trusted God's promise to Abraham, and not convinced him to impregnate their house slave, is it possible that no one would have ever cared about this place? Is it possible that

Jerusalem could have lived up to its name as the City of Peace? Maybe that's what God wanted all along. The "Promised Land" was promised to the "chosen people" before it became a city of flip-flopping massacres and before they became a people okay with killing other people.

It's time to finish. In 1187 AD, Sultan Saladin of Egypt and Syria, Ishmael's blood, led a counter crusade against the Crusaders, another holy war, or by the Muslim name, a Jihad. They won. I'm not sure why, but this is the only instance so far in this timeline that I've rooted for the losers to lose. And those are my people. But in response, "my people" had a go at another crusade. Saladin cleared out all the crops and food in the surrounding land for hundreds of miles and poisoned the wells. King Richard the Lionheart settled for a treaty with Salidin over risking the starvation of his men. The treaty allowed the Christians to visit the holy sites under Saladin's occupation. After Saladin's death in 1193 AD, a different Pope stirred up another Crusade. They failed. I think that leaves the Crusaders with a 1-2-1 record. I wonder if Jesus would be proud of them.

The Ottoman Empire took over in 1516 AD and they must have done something right because they stayed in the king spot just a year shy of four centuries until the British took over by mandate after WWI. And it was Suleiman the Magnificent of the Ottomans that built the walls we were walking. In my opinion, the fact that they're still standing says that they must be pretty magnificent walls made of bits and pieces of all the other walls that never made it.

In the 19th Century, the city was divided into quarters: the Muslim quarter, the Jewish quarter, the Christian quarter, and the Armenian quarter. It feels like a very complicated game of four-square. It's hard to say who is in the "king spot" within the walls of the Old City. The Israelis are officially in charge, their IDF are everywhere, and are watching everything. But the Muslims occupy the temple mount. The Dome of the Rock and the Al-Aqsa mosque on Mount Moriah are under Muslim control. Just like water, whoever has control of this very special spot seems to have control of the people at large. If it was up to the State of Israel, they would take over the Temple Mount today and rebuild the Temple tomorrow. They've already carved the new cornerstone out of some special rock in the Negev Desert using only hand tools. They've also built the special temple instruments and sacred objects for worship by the specific requirements found in the Old Testament. But just like the Israelis have eyes on the entire city, the world, specifically the United Nations, has eyes on them. And for now the Jewish people are going to have to wait. Later when I asked a Muslim the same question of why the Jews don't just take control of the Temple Mount, he told me that the Al-Aqsa mosque and the Dome of the Rock are considered so holy to the entire Muslim population that if they were attacked, the Muslims of the world would unite to retaliate and take back control. He said that is a war that Israel isn't prepared for, no matter with what backing, to fight.

From the top of the ramparts looking out from near the Lions Gate, you can see the Mount of Olives to the east. This hillside no longer fits its name. All the olive trees have been ripped out and replaced with dead Jews. From afar, this Jewish cemetery with over 150,000 graves looks like a slope of rocks and sand. The Mount of Olives is very familiar, but most of us couldn't remember why it was important, or exactly what had happened there. Jesus went there to walk, sit, pray, and teach. Looking out over Jerusalem, he prophesied that the Temple would be destroyed, that the Jews would be exiled, and that they would miss the true thing that would bring them peace (Luke 19:41-44). From the Mount of Olives, Jesus rode a donkey into the city and entered the Temple through the Beautiful Gate during the week of his crucifixion. And later, according to Acts 1:1-11, Jesus ascended to heaven from the Mount of Olives. The Jews have paid large sums of money to be buried in that specific cemetery because according to Old Testament prophecy in Zechariah 14, their messiah is going to come first to the Mount of Olives and then into the city through the Beautiful Gate. The idea is that they would be the first to ascend to heaven once their messiah finally comes. One hundred years ago the Jews paid the Palestinian villagers of nearby Silwan a monthly wage in hopes that they wouldn't damage the graves. The entrance gate for the Jews' messiah has been sealed off by the Muslims. Interestingly, there is another prophecy in the Jews' and Christians' Old Testament that says the gate will be sealed because the Lord has already entered through it (Ezekiel 44:1-4).

20

When we came down off the wall we walked to the Jewish Quarter for a visit to the Wailing Wall. After walking through multiple security check points, metal detectors, and having our backpacks searched, we walked through a tunnel into an open court. We were surrounded by high walls and I remember looking up to a watchtower with a feeling that I was making eye contact with the soldiers watching me through their binoculars. The guys went left and we went right. There is a divider between the men's and women's sections with chairs scattered throughout each. I walked toward the off-white limestone great wall and sat in a white plastic chair in the shade to watch. The wall is composed of huge rectangular blocks and has small cracks growing tiny shoots of greenery throughout. I wasn't sure what I was supposed to do. I sort of tried to pray, but more pretended to pray and watched others pray. There were women with their faces pressed to the wall, rubbing the rough rock with their hands. I could hear crying. Even in the shade I was sweating. I made the mistake of wiping the sweat from my forehead and somehow got sunscreen in my eyes. Now I was crying. My eyes were burning and watering, and I'm sitting at the Wailing Wall in Israel surrounded by women, some who may come here everyday and some who may have waited their entire lives for this moment. We're both crying, and I felt like a fake. I tore out a page of my tiny journal and wrote "for friendship". Then I walked up to the wall, touched it, and tried to stick my folded-up prayer in a crack alongside hundreds of other little wadded up pieces of paper of all colors. It kept falling out. Ladies were praying to my left and right, and I was just trying to get this thing to stay. I twisted it and jammed it back in praying I didn't knock a bunch of other people's sacred prayers out. It finally stayed. I started to walk away, but then I realized the other women were walking away backwards. So, I turned and started walking backwards. But then I felt like such a fake that I turned around and walked out to meet my friends.

As we were standing in the main court, I heard a man say, "Friends, come and join us." I looked over my shoulder for the Jewish people that he must have been talking to. No one was there, and again he said, "Please, join us for refreshments and cookies to celebrate Shabbat." He was an Orthodox Jew in black with a black hat, and super-long, curly sideburns. We walked to the small group of men standing around a gathering of white plastic chairs as a substitute table. We were greeted with warm handshakes and a mini-cup of soda, followed by a prayer in Hebrew and then English, a short message, and then some cookies. They were very kind to us.

Leaving there, we walked towards the Temple Mount in the Muslim Quarter. We weren't able to enter, because of the restrictions, but stood outside the city walls behind what I remember to be a short wall and looked in from a distance. Hiding in the shade of a small tree with the diesel-hum of a tour bus at my back, I realized that all the official signs in and out of the city are only for the Jewish sites. I don't blame the Muslims for not wanting to let tourists into the Dome of the Rock and the Al-Aqsa Mosque. While it has been under fire before, I'm surprised it's never been blown up. In 1968, a Jewish group built tunnels under Al-Aqsa, to try and pray closer to the original spot of the holy of holies. The UN condemned it, but they continued digging until the tunnel gave way, causing the collapse of part of the court, damage to a school, library, and 35 homes. A year later, an Australian Jew set Al-Aqsa on fire, burning the southern part of the mosque. The UN also condemned the Israeli Police Department for preventing fire engines coming from the Palestinian cities of Ramallah and Hebron. And now the City of David excavations have inched their way right up to the edge of the Temple Mount. If you look closely you can see that they're beginning to dig right beneath Al-Aqsa.

The Dome of the Rock has one of the world's largest and longest inscriptions encircling the exterior blue walls in Arabic. The inscription is made up of passages from the Quran that state that Jesus was a prophet, but he is not the Son of God. These messages along with the shape and size of the building compared to the Holy Sepulchre are said to be a very direct message for the Christians. Within the one-third of a square mile that makes up the Old City there have been many demonstrations, protests, riots, and massacres among the religious involving the city's holy sites.

Last, we walked to the Holy Sepulchre in the Christian Quarter. As we stood just outside the church and in front of its massive wooden doors, we were cleared to the side by monks in brown robes. Jon began to speak to us about the groups of Protestants and Catholics that share the responsibility of running the Sepulchre. They hate each other. They can't agree on anything. They fight over the rights to clean, down to who gets to sweep what tile. When it came to the question of who holds the key, it became a feud. The only acceptable solution was for a Muslim family to be hired to hold the key and unlock the door every morning and lock it at night. Halfway through Jon's explanation, bells started to ring from above our heads. These weren't normal bells. These were the loudest and longest bells I have ever experienced. I might as well have been inside a bell with a big crazy person hitting at it for fifteen minutes. Jon's mouth was still moving but I couldn't hear a thing. He was explaining what was inside the church. "To the right up the.... ring, ring, ring. And make sure to go down to... ring, ring, ring. Take the opportunity to be worshipful... ring, ring, ring. Remember this is where Jesus... ring, ring, ring. Meet us back here at... ring, ring, ring." *Screw it*, I thought to myself and walked into the church flustered. I ran my hand over the thick wood of the door looking for the keyhole. It was big and dark inside. And it smelled and it was hot. There were people everywhere. I went to the right and climbed the stairs. There was a line. I shuffled out of the line and sat on a stone bench against the wall. My puffer-fish feet were so swollen that when I pointed my toes up towards the really elaborate carved angels on the ceiling two folds of swollen-ness rammed into each other around what used to be my ankles. I watched. People were lined up to touch the spot where Jesus hung on the cross. There was no cross. It was a stone altar with candles on top and on the ground there was a place to crouch under and touch. It reminded me of when I was a child and I used to hide under my father's desk. I was about to get into the line again when a whole new tour bus of people showed up. I felt claustrophobic. Then I heard this monk shouting, "Madam, come here. Come here!" People were fighting in line. I remembered Jon saying, "Try to be worshipful." In my head I was trying not to cuss. Then I watched as another monk cleared away all the flowers people had left for Jesus. I didn't want to, but I got in line and slowly walked up to the spot for my turn. The lady in front of me knelt down and kissed the spot a bunch of times and rubbed her hands all over it. Then it was my turn. Again, I didn't know what to do. My brain was telling me, "Do something. This is the closest you have ever been to Jesus." And my heart said, "Jesus isn't here. This isn't his house." Standing there, I'm pretty sure I pursed my lips and gave the spot a little awkward nod, and walked away. I went back downstairs and walked around. The church is massive and it goes forever. At the other end there is a mini-capsule room in the middle of a larger cathedral-like room. This was the tomb Jesus was said to be buried in. There was a line reaching all the way round, full of at least three buses of tourists. Priests were walking around waving a metal thing hanging from a stick with smelly smoke coming out of it. And

24

as I went around the back and filed into line I notice that the line was formed by blue brigades with white letters spray-painted to say 'Jewish Police'. It felt like a really messed up version of Disneyland. I left.

We walked back to our hotel. Upon walking into the lobby I plopped down in one of the many love seats and propped my feet up. One of my good friends had moved to West Jerusalem three weeks earlier to teach at an international school for a year. This was the night we were meeting up for dinner. I told Jer, the leader of our trip and the guy that all our friends would blame if I never came home, that I was going to take a taxi to meet her at a hotel in West Jerusalem, and would take a taxi back before ten. I could tell he wasn't a big fan of my plan to leave the group on my own, but he knew I'd made up my mind, and he trusted me.

The hotel we were going to meet at was only a mile and a half away from our hotel. I could have walked, but to be on the safe side I'd just get a taxi. The thought of any more walking in the oppressive heat with my geriatric feet was repulsive. I walked to the end of the street, no taxis in sight. The next street was a one-way going the wrong direction, again no taxis. Then the traffic was so thick I continued to walk passing cars. I wasn't sure where I was going, but I had a slight idea of which direction. I got to an intersection. Many taxis. I asked, and was given an exorbitant price; I call it "white girl's price". I was told it was because prices go up on Saturday because of Shabbat, the Jewish sabbath. Even though neither I nor these Palestinian Muslim taxi drivers were Jewish. They were ripping me off at ten dollars for one mile. But they were also prideful. I could not talk them down. I got into one taxi because he said he'd charge meter. I agreed and when the door shut he punched the gas and said "Meter plus 30 shekels." I said no. Thank God for traffic, he had no choice to stop and I got out in the middle of a round-about. Flustered and angry, I decided to walk, which was something I told myself I would not do. Another taxi driver chased me down and pointed me in the right direction. I walked. As I walked further away from the east and closer to the cleaner, quieter west I began to think to myself, *"This place is not scary. The Jewish military are not scary. I have seen very few guns, and if anything the IDF bring a feeling of safety. I haven't seen anger. I didn't need my friends to pray for emotional strength. This place is fine."*

And then there was a division in the road. I remembered the direction to be 'go left'. I also remember remembering directions wrong and getting lost more often than not. So I stopped in a small corner shop to double check. I stood behind a Palestinian man speaking to the man behind the counter waiting my turn to ask my question, choosing my words, and knowing there was a good chance no one knew English. The men were speaking loudly. It seemed friendly yet edgy, like the way guys argue over sports with too much alcohol in their systems. It elevated to yelling. It was now clear these men were not friends. The man in front of me turned and abruptly walked away. Having no idea what was just said I turned towards the man at the counter to ask for directions. I was speaking, but he did not look at me. He was looking over my shoulder watching the man walking away. That's when I turned to see the same man running back in, now angry as ever, screaming in Arabic, and on his way back through the propped-open double doors he grabbed the stack of red shopping baskets by the entrance. He hurled them, right past my head, at the shopkeeper behind the counter. To get out the door I took a few quick steps back and looped behind the man now reaching over the counter and screaming his words. *What just happened?* My mind reeled as I crossed over the street to get as far away as possible. Less than a minute later, I was asked by a couple on the same street, "Do you speak English?" "Yes." "Oh, good. Do you know if it is safe to park here?" "Sorry, I don't live here. I don't know a thing."

At this point there were many turns, and I knew I had to ask. I scanned the people I was seeing to determine who was safe. I asked an older man in a suit wearing a yarmulke with the ever-so-popular, long, curly sideburns. With a New York accent and a smile he pointed me right to the hotel. As I finished my walk, I felt upset. Upset that although I had come to this place to specifically support and be open to both sides, I just picked a side. My brain told me, *If you find a nice looking Jewish person you'll be safe. Stay away from the scarier-looking Palestinians and you'll be safe.*

26

After a delightful meal with my friend, less than a month into her year-long commitment, I was quick to jump in a taxi and pay the outrageous Shabbat, white-girl price, thankful that my trip was only eleven days.

1897	**Zionist movement established**
1917	**Balfour Declaration to British Mandate**
1948	**The War of Independence Al-Nakbah "The Catastrophe" State of Israel established**
1967	**The Six-day War: Israel defeats Egypt, Syria, and Jordan**
1987	**First Intifada: Palestinian Uprising**
2000	**Second Intifada: Significant increase of violence and killings**
2005	**Barrier wall established to divide West Bank and State of Israel**

day three

The breakfast was the same for the third day running- hummus, veggies, bread, bologna, and instant coffee. Even though this was my third day of no caffeine and jet lag, I refused to drink instant coffee. When I sat down at the table with my plate of cherry tomatoes I was greeted by, "Where were you last night? Didn't you hear the fire alarm at 3am?" I vaguely remembered waking up to some very loud beeping and then rolling over and going back to sleep. Not a smart move on my part, or Carli's, who was also in my room. I blame the fact that I've grown accustomed to ignoring my roommates alarm clocks in our paper-thin walled house. Apparently, Jer, in the room next to me, got up, checked the hall for smoke, soaked his towel in the sink, and ran down to the lobby in his boxers ready to put out a fire with his wet hotel towel. I was told this by the rest of our group who heeded the alarm, and were also down in the lobby at 3am. Jer and I have very different approaches to fire alarms.

The goal of this day was to hear and try to understand the Jewish side of this story. We would spend the day with twenty-seven year-old Liel. He would accompany us in the afternoon to Yad Vashem, Israel's Holocaust museum, and in the evening, back at the hotel, we would get to hear his story.

Six months before my trip, my ground-level knowledge of the Jewish people was very basic. It's embarrassing, stereotypical, and borderline racist, but here's an honest inside look to what my brain thought when it came to Jews. Jews are financially savvy,

29

wear little hats, have dark curly hair and the overly religious ones have very extremely long sideburns. Jews were very legalistic when it came to laws and traditions of their religion and really didn't like Jesus in Biblical times. And of course they suffered the horrific injustice of the Holocaust. It was also always confusing to me whether they were an ethnicity, a religion, or a nationality.

Since then I have learned that the Jews are an extraordinary people, an absolutely extraordinary group of people. Their story is one of resilience, commitment, adaptation, and perseverance in the midst of trial. Their story is also traumatic. They are a people who, generation after generation, faced traumatizing circumstances. They are a people who suffer from cultural PTSD (post-traumatic stress syndrome). That means that their children grow up hearing stories that ingrain in them this thought, *Because you are a Jew, people hate you. People want to kill you. We have to fight for the right to stay.* When I was a child, before bed my mother read me stories about puppies and friendly octopuses. In order to understand Jews in Israel today and their thought process behind the occupation and the walls, it's important to take a second deeper look back into their history.

Again, I've heard the best place to start is at the beginning. Jewish history and the history of Jerusalem run in the same circles. In Canaan, God offered Abraham a covenant and a promise if he circumcised himself and changed his allegiance to one God instead of many. Abraham and Sarah had their last minute-miracle child, who trumped poor Ishmael. With Ishmael kicked out of town, Isaac started his own family. His son Jacob had tons of sons, and got his name changed by God to Israel. Israel's twelve sons led the twelve tribes of Israel who settled in Canaan, also known as the promised land, later known as Palestine, and currently known as Israel and the West Bank.

After the Israelites migrated to Egypt to the escape famine they were eventually enslaved by the Egyptians. According to the Old Testament, after 400 years of slavery, the prophet Moses was sent to the Israelites to lead them out of slavery in Egypt and back to the promised land in Canaan. To most, the ten plagues and the Israelites' exodus from Egypt are familiar Bible stories. It was the tenth and final plague, the killing of all the first-born sons in Egypt, that gives us the tradition of Passover. The Israelites were told to spread the blood from a lamb over their doorposts so that the spirit of death would pass over their homes, sparing their first-borns. A common saying before a present-day Passover meal, or Sader dinner, is "They tried to kill us, but we survived, let's eat." But the Passover meal's true purpose is to celebrate God's provision and the fact that He never abandoned or abandons the Jewish people.

After the baby slaughter plague, the Pharaoh released the Israelites, and under Moses' lead they wandered the Sinai Desert for forty years. It was in that time that Moses climbed up Mount Sinai and received the Ten Commandments and a lot of other rules, promises, and threats. Just before he led them back to the 'promised land' (it was literally in view) Moses stood on a hill looking out onto the goal of his entire life and then God came right up to him. After seeing His face, it was there that he died, just a few steps short of the be all end all. This is interesting to me. What if the be all end all isn't actually the 'promised land'? What if the be all end all isn't the Mount Moriah/Temple Mount/Dome of the Rock spot? What if the be all end all isn't rubbing a wall, or squatting under an altar, or visiting a place where someone really important walked a really long time ago? What if the be all end all was actually the act of standing before the face of God?

Joshua and Caleb took up the reins and led the Israelites to conquer the Jebusites and took back the 'promised land'. It was there that they became organized. They had judges who split up the land among the tribes, and eventually instead of letting God be king of their non-political people group, they convinced God to let them have a human king. We go from King Saul, to David, to Solomon, and we get a city and a temple. In the Temple go the Ten Commandments and the Ark of the Covenant, and the religion of the Israelites comes to order according to their oral traditions and texts. The laws of the Torah cover every part of life. And they were a people dedicated to the law. After King Solomon's death, the twelve tribes waged war on each other, becoming the Kingdom of Israel in the north and Judah in the south. After the Assyrians conquered the City of David, the Israelites scattered and intermarried among tribes. When Judah was conquered two centuries later by Babylon, many of their people joined with other dispersed Israelites and began to refer to themselves as a race of people called the Jews (people of Judah) and settled in the area around Jerusalem. The Hebrews (pre-Israelites) go from a religious people, to Israelites who were a religious nation, to Jews who were a wandering, religious race.

When the Babylonians destroyed the temple, the Jewish people were again exiled, dispersed to other areas and many were taken to be slaves in Babylon. On their way out, the prophet Jeremiah told them, "Have a lot of babies and plant a lot of crops, because you will return." It was in Babylon that their scribes became dedicated to writing down their entire oral history and compiling the majority of the written Torah, the first five books of the Bible. This is when they truly became "people of the book". The Jews became a people governed not by the laws of the place they inhabited, but by the laws of their religion. And wherever they went, wherever they were exiled to or from, they took their laws and religion with them and lived in community. The religion of the Jews promised that if they meticulously followed the laws they would be blessed and eventually come out on top. And that is why they never disappeared. That is why they still exist. They are people willing to dedicate their lives to religion in the midst of suffering, in hopes of the promise of something better.

In come the Persians to wipe out the Babylonians, and the Jews are reinstated in Jerusalem. They are allowed to build a second temple, thus strengthening their people, their religion, and their culture. And 600 years later when their temple was destroyed by the Romans, they were exiled again. But this was not the end for them. The Rabbis decided that the end of the temple and the end of the land didn't have to mean the end of the people. They entered into a new phase of Jewish life, and spread through the Roman Empire. Under Rome's widespread peace treaty, the Pax Romana, the Jews migrated to Asia minor (Turkey and Italy), North Africa, and Mesopotamia (Iraq). In these places they continued to live communally, governed by their own laws. And with no more temple and no more messages from prophets, Rabbinic Judaism began. They replaced the temple rituals with prayers at the synagogues. The Biblical period of prophecy was

32

considered finished, and it was now time to study. From this point on, access to God came only through the scribe, the sage, and the rabbi.

The Jews continued to be persecuted when the Roman Empire adopted Christianity as their official religion. They were forbidden to build synagogues, testify in court, or read the Hebrew Bible in public. And eventually with Rome out and the Islamic Army in, within a hundred years of the start of Islam, Muslims were in control of 80-90 percent of the Jewish population. For the most part, the Jews were allowed to settle and had freedom of religion under Islam, but not always. As Jews continued to migrate and spread there became two main groups of Jews. The Sephardic were the Jews of Spain, Portugal, North Africa, and the Middle East. And the Ashkenazi were the Jews of France, Germany, and Eastern Europe.

In 711 AD the Muslim Moors gained control of Spain and invited the Jews to come live and worship freely among them. The Jews of Spain, the Sephardim, lived for 400 years in this place without massacres and exiles. This time period is called the Golden Age because within their communities and amongst their Spanish neighbors, they flourished. They not only held tightly to their own culture, religion, and tradition, but they also adapted and embraced the culture in which they lived. Their economic expansion during this period was unparalleled. They also made great contributions to society through academics, medicine, botany, and the arts. This period ended when anti-Semitism reared its ugly, big head during the Crusades. At this same time, the Ashkenazi Jews were spreading out in communities throughout Europe. Eventually, they lost the Hebrew language and began to speak Yiddish, a mash-up of Hebrew, Aramaic, and German infused with Romance languages.

The Christians have been historically more horrible to the Jews than the Muslims were. Christians massacred thousands of Jews during the Crusaders' holy rampage march. After the Crusades and the expulsions from France, England, and Germany, the Jews migrated East to Poland and Russia. Poland and Russia actually invited them in because they were trying to populate the land. And there they lived for almost 600 years without too much commotion. They were able to live and allowed to govern themselves. They weren't rich, they weren't poor, and they weren't without persecution, but they survived generation after generation.

The Spanish Inquisition in the 1400s was another "holy act" of the Christians. It boils down to the Christians saying to the Muslims and the Jews, "Accept Jesus into your heart or get out." There is a pattern here. The Jews get somewhere, they set up camp just long enough to start doing their thing, and then people start to notice. People start to notice that their "thing", whatever it is that they were doing, is working. Acting on insecurities, inferiority, and fear, they either kill them or kick them out. The second piece of the same pattern is religious people killing other religious people under an umbrella of holy justification.

This brings us to the late 1800s and the birth of Zionism. Following the American Revolution and the Enlightenment, slowly but surely many countries were emancipating the Jewish community, and the Jews were experiencing new liberties and freedoms. This new period of open thinking sparked ideas and dreams of migrating to a place that could provide a better life for their people. There were waves of Ashkenazi Jews immigrating from Europe to America and Sephardic Jews immigrating out of the declining Ottoman Empire. A new "old" idea surfaced, the solution to the great Jewish problem, a return to the promised land, the historic Kingdom of Israel, in Palestine.

Author, Theodor Herzl, wrote his book, *Judenstadt* or "Jewish State" in 1896. It was pushing for the Jews to fight for their own state. He believed that the solution for the Jews, now spread out across the world and victim to fierce persecution and anti-Semitism, was to move to a safe place of their own. His book was basically the manifesto for Zionism, a return the 'promised land'. There were some light waves of immigration, but the idea and the Zionist dream didn't take off and flourish as Herzl had hoped.

Twenty million people died in World War I between 1914 and 1918. At the war's end, the world longed for peace like never before. Russia outlawed anti-Semitism and the Communists and Socialists proclaimed equality. America became a super-power, and its allies in Europe took control and colonized much of the Ottoman Empire. The British took Palestine and under their mandate they approved establishing a national Jewish home in Palestine, giving them the rights to just over half the land. There were small waves of immigration, or *Aliyahs*, to Palestine causing riots among the Palestinians who were losing their land and homes. Soon after, things turned dark with leaders like Stalin and Hitler. Hitler led Germany, fresh off an epic loss in WWI, in targeting the Jews and resurrect the country's superiority. Europe's Ashkenazi Jews experienced a roller coaster ride from freedom and flourishing to experiencing perhaps the most large-scale act of evil and hate in our world's history, the Holocaust.

The Holocaust is what we know most. There is an addictive curiosity about this event in history, similar to the way we can't help but slow down on the highway to look at terrible car wrecks. There are many who want to commemorate and give value to the stories of those who were killed. Words like horrific, evil, atrocity, systematic-murder, emaciated, torture, children, suffering, and hopelessness, and pictures of piles of shoes, mass graves, and living, skin-and-bone slave worker adults and children- I imagine these do absolutely no justice in describing what it felt like to be there. The feeling of being the recipient of hate worth mass-murder. Six million died feeling it, and just over a million survived feeling it. And the Jewish people for the rest of time will feel it in a way that words and pictures fail to describe.

On the bus to Yad Vashem I looked out the window to see a crosswalk sign in West Jerusalem that had a Hassidic Jew stick-man wearing a black hat. When we got to the museum there were groups of teenage IDF soldiers waiting in large groups in the lobby. They checked their weapons at the same desk where we checked our backpacks. Not unlike us, they were on a field trip to the second most popular site in Israel, behind the Wailing Wall. I wondered what the experience of walking through a Holocaust museum would be like for a fresh-out-of-bootcamp soldier about to embark on a two year right of passage to protect his country. I couldn't shake the thought, *These are their people*

*who were murdered, and this is their state that they are about to
defend so that this may never happen again.*

The museum was cold, mostly concrete, perfected down to the
detail, and near silent. We spent four hours with headphones,
slowly walking and taking in as much horror as our insides were
capable of. I was constantly aware of what the Jews around me
might have been feeling as they heard, saw, and were reminded
of what I was seeing. Again, part of me felt like an imposter,
being somewhere I didn't belong. Yet, I didn't skim and scan,
instead I read, and then I read again. I wanted to understand.

I wrote down quotes.

"This was a painful, surprising betrayal by a culture on which I
had pinned all my hopes, to which I had devoted all my
admiration, my heartfelt adoration. A betrayal I may have partly
been anticipating, but here it has been confirmed with such
brutality... All of Europe has turned into a monster."

-Albert Memmi

"Leszno Street, the main street in the Ghetto. Cut off at both
ends. Full of people at every turn, no segment is without masses
of people, traffic and screams. Everywhere noise and
commotion, everywhere crowded..."
-Israel Gutman, underground newspaper April 1941

"I am calm now, destined to be killed."
-Journal of Margaret

Another group's tour guide quoted Stalin, "The death of an
individual is a tragedy. The death of one million people is just a
statistic.", as we were standing over a massive pile of shoes
under glass. Then he said, "The shoes. Look at the shoes. If
you look closely you can see a few blue shoes and even a red
shoe. They are not all the same."

"All of us, dying here amidst the icy arctic indifference of the
nations, are forgotten by the world and by life..."
-Camp inmate Avraham Levite, 1945

36

"At the very end were the death marches. Three months of walking through snow with no food or water. We walked over 800km. I thought our neighbors would never do this to us."
- A Holocaust survivor

"They tried to kill us, yet we still exist."
-Anonymous

"The victory is ours."
This was engraved in large letters into concrete pillars, framing a breathtaking outlook onto Jerusalem. As I exited the museum I was struck by the motto, by the view, and with a wall of heat. Walking away there was a new quote echoing in my head, not sure if I had thought it up or heard it from one of my friends, but it lingered, and it's still lingering.

"Where there is no reconciliation, history will repeat itself."

It was a long, quiet bus ride home. Once back to the hotel, my friends and I strolled back into the Old City from our hotel to find a roof-top restaurant where we began to unpack all we had seen and heard. Liel had been with us all day. I like him. He fit with us, being a twenty-something in somewhat scruffy clothes, quick to smile, and soft-spoken. He is a Jew born in Israel, who after serving his two years in the Army, began to question his government and the occupation. Now he works for an organization that is dedicated to creating dialog between Israelis and Palestinians. He works in tourism in order to educate those who visit by sharing both Israeli and Palestinian narratives and perspectives. We sat together around a table of beers and frozen minty lemonades and Liel shared with us about his life. This is his story.

"My name is Liel Maghen and my family has lived in Rome for the last twelve generations. They were more Italian than Jewish before the Holocaust. My grandmother was actually half-Christian. My grandfather wanted to propose to my grandmother before the war. But my grandmother's father said it would have to wait until after the war, and if my grandfather survived he could propose. During the Holocaust because my grandmother was half-Christian she and her brother were hidden in monasteries in Rome. My grandfather's story is quite inspirational. He ran away to the south of Italy. While he was on the run my grandfather was in an open field, and he saw a vision of his uncle who had been dead for ten years. His uncle said to him, "Go over there one kilometer and dig, you'll find water and food. Leave this place now because airplanes are going to fly over and shoot this spot." And that's exactly what happened.

Another time the Germans were chasing him and he got to a cliff over a river, and jumped. The British Army was at the bottom, and took him from the water. He joined the British Army, and they conquered Italy. He was one of the first Jews to enter back into Rome. And the very first thing he did was to go straight to my grandmother's house and propose. Soon after they were married.

After the war their family became very religious. They started to go to synagogue, visited Israel more, and talked about the importance of the Jewish state. They often talked about the importance of keeping the religion because many people had died. My grandfather started praying three times a day. They kept the holidays and Sabbath. And my grandmother began to eat kosher. Every time they came to visit, they'd go straight to *the Wailing Wall, and put a note in it to thank God that they were saved.*

The Holocaust changed every Jewish family that suffered through it. For many it was a lot worse than it was for my grandparents. Many people lost ninety percent of their family. For them, all they have are pictures. A lot of our people don't know their family at all. It also brought up questions. What are you? What do you represent? What do you want to do with your religion? And it brought up disappointment in the local people, a disappointment in their neighbors. They saw themselves as truly Italian. They were so confident in their country and trusted their government, they didn't think that they would be affected or needed to run away. But eventually that's what life brought to them, and the locals who turned on them didn't feel the same.

It is important to understand the split in the way many Jews regard the Holocaust. My grandfather talks about it a lot, but my grandmother doesn't talk about it. Many don't want to remember it at all. They don't want it to be part of the present, saying it belongs to the past. The other side wants to commemorate it. Many want it to be a major subject in school because it is an important lesson. From my grandfather I heard a lot of stories. From my grandmother I heard nothing. We need to remember that there are always two groups. One who wants to talk and one who wants to leave it in the past.

Currently it has become popular for the younger generation of secular upper class Jews to apply for European passports to go back and live in the places where their families lived before the Holocaust. Many of the grandparents are completely against it and tell their grandchildren that it is insulting to them. They ran away from those countries, and want no connection to them.

There is a third group of people. Unlike my grandparents who became more connected to their faith, many people became secular. Not only were they disappointed in their neighbors, they were disappointed in God. Because of the WWII they didn't believe in the religion any more. Because of the Holocaust they believed God must not exist.

In 1951, under great pressure from the US and the UN, the Germans began to pay for what they had done. To date, the German government has paid over 50 billion dollars in reparation payments to compensate for slave labor, the killing of innocent civilians, and stolen and seized property. Ninety percent of the money went to the government, and in the fifties, the payments made up to 80 percent of Israel's total income. Israel as a state officially forgave the Germans and took advantage of having ties to Germany and Europe. With Europe supporting Israel, the new enemy became the Arabs. The inflow of money quickly separated the Israelis from the Palestinians. Jews were getting money for just being Jews, so the infrastructure of the two cultures became dramatically different.

Once Israel as a state forgave Europe, then the people began to forgive as well. The people who had been Europeans all their lives began to feel free to act like Europeans again, but they wanted to do it here. Now you see different pockets of people representing different European cultures in places like Tel-aviv and Jerusalem. For Germans and Russian Jews it was very hard to come to Israel. It had a different climate, traditions, and the people weren't as kind and hospitable. When the country forgave Germany, they felt more comfortable being like what they were before the Holocaust, and reclaiming some of their identity. They stayed in their communities grouped by their European cultures because it provided a feeling of safety.

In 1960, the Israeli Secret Service captured one of Hitler's high-ups, Adolf Eichmann, who fled to Argentina at the Holocaust's end. They brought him to Jerusalem and put him on trial. The trial sparked widespread interest among the public. Among a long list of charges, Adolf was charged with coordinating and implementing the death camps down to the last detail and seizing of Jewish property and assets to his own benefit. Eichmann was convicted and put to death in 1962. It was the many testimonies that first put words to the horrific atrocities against the Jews that seemed to allow the Jewish population to start talking about the Holocaust ten years later.

In high school we have a whole year where we study the Holocaust. And at the end of the year we go on a trip to Europe to the death camps. When I visited Germany for the first time, I *felt afraid. It is the psychology of feeling scared because of things that we learn. Especially for my generation when the grandparents don't forgive.*

My father was born in Libya, which was colonized by Italy. Because he knew Italian, he later moved to Italy. He worked in the Jewish Agency, a zionist organization. His work was to recruit Jews from Europe to migrate to Israel. It was something really Zionist to do, something to be really proud of. Because he spent so much time talking about why it was so important to move here, eventually he was convinced to move his family too. My father and his family didn't suffer from the Holocaust, because they were in North Africa. But because the Holocaust became so central in Israeli conversation, I think they felt like they needed to prove their persecution. Because the cost was so high to move, family, friends, home, possessions, culture, identity... it seemed important to prove your persecution even to yourself.

The Holocaust was one of the main reasons why the Israeli state was established, and the main reason why the UN voted in favor of it. There is a Holocaust day. It sits inbetween Passover, Memorial Day, and Independence Day. It is an entire week of commemorating our national identity. Our theme, being something like- "People try to kill us, we survive, and now we establish a state."
Every year all the movies during this week on the television are about the Holocaust. As a child I remember seeing this and feeling very scared. Sometimes as a child it's really horrifying to see these pictures or to hear these stories. They stay in your mind. I remember I had many nightmares. They became so many I started to believe that I was a victim of the Holocaust in a different life, and now I am resurrected as an Israeli being or something. It became part of my identity. When I was older it became even more central. At age 13 we do something called "roots paperwork" in school. We have to go and find our roots. We research our families, where we came from, and it all comes back to the Holocaust. Then for the entire year we study a lot about Naziism and the Holocaust. The year before I was drafted into the army, I went to Poland for a trip to a death camp and the concentration camp. The Holocaust is always central in our education system; it is our national identity. A lot of people

migrate from all around the world to Israel, and the only thing everyone shares in common is the fact everyone has been persecuted. When I got back from Poland they emphasized that going into the army and being patriotic was the solution and the modern defense against the second Holocaust. Joining the army is the conclusion of the Holocaust. They made these connections all the time. But not everyone gets this.

Things happened to me in the army that caused me to question what I was doing. In my time in the Army I was drafted to a combat unit. They told me, "Liel, you need to guard a prisoner. He is very dangerous. You need to guard him carefully. Be on guard, he's very, very dangerous." And I remember that because of all my emotions about the Holocaust, and my education, and the importance of the army, I went to do this mission with pride. I thought to myself, "Ya, now I'm the Israel hero. This is my role, and it's my time to defend my state. However, when I got there I saw a twelve-year-old kid with his hands tied behind his back, and his eyes covered. But when I was there I felt that he was dangerous. They told me he was, so surely he is. It is only now I look back and see how twisted it was to look at it this way. Especially after I went into education I understood that twelve-year-old kids need good education and support or else they will pick up stones.

Another experience I had was when I was told again, "Liel, you need to guard someone. He is dangerous." But when I got there he was in an ambulance, and he had been shot. He was badly injured, and I went to the hospital with him. A few hours into the ride, I remember I looked into his eyes, and he looked into mine. In this twisted mind I thought he was dangerous, and I stayed on guard with my weapon. Even though he couldn't have done anything. He was shot. He couldn't even move.

Only later when I was released from the army, I traveled the world and spoke with people who weren't in the army. It was then that I began to question this and realize how strange and awkward these lessons were. And how in that moment the most important thing for me was to obey the order, and not question it. But the real lesson of our history and the Holocaust is to question the order. When I discovered this I decided to try and change my life. I did education and dedicated my life to meeting

42

with Palestinians, and now I'm connected to different Israeli/Palestinian dialogues and projects. The idea is to correct our perspective by understanding someone else's perspective.

Here is a story that happened yesterday, here in Jerusalem. There were two young Arab guys that walked into the center of Jerusalem only five minutes from here, and then around 40-50 Jewish people came to them and yelling, "Arabs you shouldn't be here!" They beat them up. Both of the Palestinians are in the hospital, and one is in a coma. The night before, a settler threw a Molotov cocktail explosive into a Palestinian taxi close to a settlement nearby here. The driver was badly burned and is now at the same hospital as the two boys. These actions are part of a larger phenomenon of a Jewish hatred toward Arabs. You'll see during your week here that it is the outcome of the violent attacks toward Israelis. But at the root is still hatred. Our government is creating laws that are different for Jews and Palestinians. There is a genocide in Sudan, and their refugees are coming to our borders. Israel doesn't accept refugees. Although many Sudanese manage to get in, they are slowly deported. You can hear the Israeli ministers say, "Refugees are a cancer. We want only a Jewish state. Everyone else should be deported." The connection between these stories is they are all the outcome of not understanding the real lesson of the Holocaust. When I went to Washington DC to the Holocaust museum, it talks about all the ethnicities and groups that were deported and persecuted as well. And they talk about other genocides that happen in other countries. Here, you will only hear of our persecution. As if we are the only ones who need defending.

Why do people repeat crimes? In a specific moment it seems the most natural thing to do. I don't want to be a criminal, I don't want to go to jail, so I'll do it. My friends are guarding in the West Bank, and they really feel in danger. They really feel like it's the right thing to do, and they believe in why we do it. Nazis were the same way. It's only after you look back with a different perspective that you are able to see that it was wrong. In all the Nuremberg trials, the Nazis all said, "It was what I was ordered to do."

I heard a saying, "War is when old people are arguing, and young people are dying."

If terror is creating fear, who are the real terrorists? Is it the people with the bomb or the government?

Because every Israeli goes into the army; we are all taught to obey. Again, I think the most important lesson from the Holocaust is to question your government. The Germans did what they were supposed to do by law. They were considered criminals if they did not obey. But, the people we remember the most and inspire the most are the ones who didn't want to obey. Nelson Mandela, Gandhi, and Martin Luther King saw that the laws were immoral. If we are able to transform the real lessons of the Holocaust and to make them the center of education, I believe only then we can create a true conflict solution.

The Holocaust and the Israeli/Palestinian conflict are the two most sensitive topics in Israel. They are like two time bombs in every conversation. When I try to talk about them with my new perspective it creates tension and conflict. Especially with my family and my father. For them I was questioning their identity, and the land, and everything they believe in. But with my friends it has been easier. I slowly, slowly share new arguments, perspectives, and questions. Last Christmas I took some friends to Bethlehem in the West Bank. It was their first time as tourists and not soldiers. They knew it by day, but not by night. And it was amazing for them. They felt confident and secure, and now they don't want to do reserves in the West Bank. It's small steps, slowly, slowly. Some people are open, but some people react very badly. I've been called a traitor many times, and other things like self-hating Jew, and told I should leave the country. It doesn't offend me anymore. It's part of creating a change.

This change started happening to me in the army, and then when I went traveling abroad. When I traveled, somehow I managed to make close friends with Iranians, Lebanese, and Palestinians, by chance really; we happened to be going to the same places in India. And when I got back here a seed was in my mind and my heart. And then by coincidence a friend asked me to join her in a dialogue project. It wasn't really a decision, I just went. But I enjoyed it. And I felt like somehow it was completing a missing part in me, something that was obscured, something that was negative and painful; I had managed to find the medicine for it.

44

And I continued in it, from one dialogue project to another, and then I led one. Then I studied in an international school. Now I study political science, and work for a peace-building non-profit alongside Palestinians. I'm learning Arabic. Every time I move forward in these things, I take another step towards living in coexistence. As a matter of fact, as I walked to your hotel today I was thinking about how the first time I ever walked here was one year ago. I was really scared. But today I am not scared, I know my way around, and I know some people. Conflict resolution is about small daily steps, where you eat your food, where you get your coffee, who you walk with, and what you talk about. Small steps. Small steps show people a different way of behaving. A different way of living. When you do this, people are inspired, and if they aren't inspired at least they see that it is an option.

I'm not sure if I'd call it passion, but it's almost like being addicted to it. When I know Palestinians, when I know what it is like to walk in the peace bubble, I can't go back. It's like I kind of know the truth right now. It's almost like finding religion. It's how I want to live. This is what I am. This is how I want to educate my kids. I want this to be my identity more than who I was before. I believe in what I am doing right now, right now in this current moment today. The belief is what keeps me connected. Depending on belief is what gives us hope. The beauty of narrative is that it changes. I can shape the narrative according to what I feel is more powerful and more important. It's not something that's frozen. It's not something that belongs only to the past. It can change everyday. What do you want to tell? What do you want to create for the people that listen to you? What do you want to create to tell yourself? My narrative or my side of the story could be, "I'm persecuted. Muslims hate me, Christians hate me. I can't live abroad because there will be a second Holocaust." Or something different. "I am part of humanity. Humanity is making mistakes across the world. Humanity did some mistakes towards my people, and my people have done mistakes to part of humanity." This can be my narrative."

day four

After a solid night of sleep lacking fire alarms and all night Muslim street parties, we were met by Husam at breakfast. Husam, much like Liel, has studied and daily lives out conflict resolution and peace building. He lives in the West Bank and would be the one to guide and narrate our time there within its walls. Before we left the hotel we sat down with Husam, and he shared his experience of life in the West Bank as a Palestinian man.

"My name is Husam Jubran and I grew up in Beit Sehour near Bethlehem, known to Christians as the shepherd's fields. I wasn't active or involved in politics when I was a kid. I was afraid to be around or even near people who spoke about politics. We were afraid to mention the word Palestine. If you were found with a Palestinian flag you could spend six months in prison. I was terrified to talk politics because I didn't want to have problems with Israelis. I knew if I got myself into trouble with them it would affect my chances of getting an education. And school was my way out. I remember

when I was 16, people would come to our school and try and convince us to strike. I refused to talk to them. But, in 1987 when the First Intifada began, I don't know how or even why, but I found myself in the streets throwing stones at the Israeli Army. To be honest the first time we picked up those stones it felt fun. And from there I became very active in demonstrations and throwing stones. Eventually, I became well known by the Israeli Army. Six months later, they came and arrested me just after my seventeenth birthday. I stayed in prison for six months and for the first 54 days I was in interrogation. It was a very hard process; for those 54 days I showered three times and was never allowed to change my clothes. When the interrogations were over I was sentenced for six months and moved to three different prisons. And the moment I was released it didn't take me more than three seconds, and I was back on the streets with my friends throwing stones at the Israeli Army. Why? I don't know. I continued being active and then I realized that soon they would come and arrest me. It was then I decided I wouldn't give myself up and make the same mistake as before. We stayed awake at night, we avoided the soldiers, and we kept watch. Beit Sahour is known for the fact that we were the first area during the First Intifada to stop paying taxes to the Israelis. We started the same campaign found in America's history, "No taxation without representation". Almost everyone in the town refused to pay taxes and we gave our identification cards back. It was a progressive act of civil disobedience, and the Israelis took it very seriously. I knew they would come and arrest me. And when they did come there were 17 of us who ran away. Ten of our 17 gave themselves up the next day. And myself and six others became fugitives. Our wanted pictures were put up around town. For three years I was wanted, and I stayed in different houses each night to avoid being caught. If it felt risky, we would go out and sleep in the caves and sometimes we hid in a monastery. At times it was fun and exhilarating. There was something very special about the way that all the people of our town were always helping us. We had nothing, so people would give us food, and places to stay. Always there was someone to help us. Even some people gave us the keys to their houses so we'd have a safe place to stay.

One day I was recognized by an Israeli soldier, and he shot me. He was shooting to kill but missed his target. I spent three months in the hospital, and still was able to avoid arrest during that time. When the peace process started and the Intifada began to cease, we thought it was over. We thought it was safe to stop hiding. We were driving in the city and were stopped and arrested. But we were only in prison for 18 days, which was strange because we had been wanted for so long.

After I was released I decided to refocus my attention on my education. After finishing high school, I couldn't attend university because all of the universities were closed by the military between 1988-1990. When the schools reopened in 1991 I studied social work at Bethlehem University. After finishing, instead of working as a social worker I decided to go back to school to be a tour guide. After completing that program I couldn't get a permit to drive tours outside of the West Bank because I was blacklisted. So, I worked a day here and there within the West Bank. In 1999, I was able to get my name off the blacklist and guided religious tours. But it wasn't fulfilling to me. I felt like a recorder on repeat. I shifted to something that mattered to me, working with political groups and tours. In 2001, the situation became very hard with the Second Intifada, and I tried very hard to find a way to leave. Later that year I got married, but my wife was from Jerusalem and I was from Bethlehem. But without permits, and because of the wall and the check points, there was no way we could be together. So, I decided again to focus on education. I got a scholarship for a masters program in conflict management and peace building in Virginia. With a masters, I began to train students in non-violence solutions at the local university. Now my passions are non-violence and tourism. I continue to facilitate non-violent leadership and communication skills trainings, and guide dual narrative tours."

In order to understand why a seventeen year-old boy became a fugitive for throwing stones at an army, we need context. In order to understand why a man with a college degree needs to apply for a permit to drive outside his town, we need context. And in order to understand why a husband and wife are forced to live in separate houses in separate towns, we need context.

Our context begins with the world's reaction and solution to the Holocaust, and those it left behind. The League of Nations, now the United Nations, approved a partition plan to divide Palestine into two states after the war's end. It gave just over fifty-seven percent of the country to the control of the Zionists and displaced Jews who would immigrate back to their original "promised land". The slogan was: "Giving a people without a land to a land without a people." The problem with this slogan is the land had a people- the Palestinians. In 1947, before the partition plan, the Palestinians made up 70% of the population and lived on 95% of the land. The world was willing to displace 750,000 of the 1.4 million Arabs in Palestine in order to compensate the displaced Jews.

If someone knocked on your door and said, "Leave. Leave now.", what would you do? I'd say, "No, this is my home." And then I'd shut the door. Of course the Palestinians rejected the Partition Plan. Not only did they reject the plan, but they began to riot against the Jews who had already immigrated. No doubt they knew war was coming, but they could have never known its outcome. If they knew the prison they'd be forced to live in today, maybe they would have accepted the two-state solution.

The British were in control of Palestine before and during WWII, but when the war was over they pulled out of the country. The British pulling out and Israel being declared a state were simultaneous. And on the same day that Israel was granted its independence the surrounding Arab nations attacked. This is known as the War of Independence by the Jews and Al-Nakbah, or "The Catastrophe" by the Palestinians. Though Israel was small, they had a strong military presence. Ben Gurion, the first Israeli Prime minister, relied on rogue soldiers from existing underground Jewish military organizations to join forces with the men who had recently immigrated, to build a defense against the Arabs. With smaller numbers they were able to win the war because unlike the Arabs, they were organized and had clear leadership. With their victory, they expanded to take even more land than the the League of Nations had allocated. What this means is during and after the war Israeli armed men knocked on thousands of Palestinian doors and said, "Leave." Imagine 7 out of every 10 men, women, and children in the state of Rhode Island evicted from their towns and their homes, with only what their arms can hold, aimlessly walking towards Connecticut. That is the picture of the Palestinians' new reality after the Al-Nakba in 1948.

After hearing Husam's story, we loaded the bus, left East Jerusalem, and headed to the ruins of a Palestinian village. I didn't actually know where we were going. Honestly, I never knew where we were going. I tended to get on the bus, follow the person in front of me, and be sure to have my sunglasses, water, and passport. We pulled off the road and got off the bus at what appeared to be an overlook. Husam pointed down, "Come, we are walking down now." It was a super steep and almost non-existent path. The ground was crumbly. If I could go back I would have advised myself not to wear flip-flops that day. But in my own defense my options were slim considering the size of my plump porker ankles. With arms fully extended for balance I shuffled and baby-stepped my way down to Lufta with only a handful of "*Oh Shit*!", almost falls. The houses that scattered the hillside were beautiful and made of pale stone. Many of the abandoned houses had two stories and intricately cut stones that framed the window and doors. Husam explained that this was a thriving and affluent Palestinian village made rich by the invention of stone cutting. They were a village of architects, builders, and those who could afford the best.

As we stood in the shade of a tree next to the village's water hole, built up like a pool, there was laughter. A handful of Israeli children had made the trek down from who-knows-where, to jump from the high side of built up stone down into the not-so-clean water, over and over again. I imagine that the scene we were watching was a very similar one to what the Palestinian children of Lufta did 65 years before. In the presence of laughter and child's play we learned that it was probable the people of Lufta heard about the horrific massacre of men, women and children in the village of Deri Asin, and fled their homes for somewhere safer, leaving everything, "even dinner on the table". The villagers that fled throughout Palestine expected to return to their homes in a few days or weeks when the war was over. However, they have never been allowed to return. Their houses still stand, yet all their belonging have been taken, and still to this day their land and their homes lie in an area that Palestinians have no access to. But I was free to go there. I had no problem visiting desolate and beautiful Lufta, other than a poor choice of footwear, because I was born in Florida. Not because of who I am, but because of who I am not. No doubt many of the same Palestinian children from Lufta who spent the hottest days of the summer jumping into a swimming hole grew up to throw rocks in the West Bank.

Where did all the Palestinians go? We got back onto the bus; Husam was taking us there. We passed through a checkpoint with ease and entered back into the West Bank. Again, we were far off the tourist track and our little bus stopped off another small road and parked us in the shadow of the wall. In the West Bank and in most parts of Israel, when one says "the wall" there is no confusion to which wall is being spoken of. The intimidating, concrete-sectioned wall weaves and snakes over

the land as far as the eye can see. Husam walked us out to a spot know as Everest that overlooked all of Bethlehem and parts of Jerusalem below us. With no shade to be found, squinting, my eyes were drawn to two things, the "temporary" wall and the black cylinder water tanks on every roof. You need extra tanks to store water when it gets cut off for months at a time. The land is beautiful, but it was hard to see past the ugly.

Why is there a wall? There is a wall because eventually it went from stones to bombs. During the Second Intifada, which began in 2000, the disorganized Palestinians revolted and started blowing up buses and themselves in crowded areas. Suicide bombers, men and woman, strapped on vests loaded with nails, shrapnel, and dynamite and exploded themselves in busy marketplaces and squares filled with men, women, and children. In the West Bank, there are shrines to these people. Their portraits can be found graffitied onto the wall. Many Muslims, but not all, consider them martyrs and heroes. I was told by a Muslim friend here in the States that part of the Muslim belief is that every Muslim has a responsibility to stand up to injustice no matter what the cost. For instance, in the Muslim culture under Muslim rule if a murderer is caught, the family of the victim is given the right to kill the murderer. They can choose to forgive and spare his life, which is looked on as noble, but it is rare and not expected. There are extremist Muslims that hold to this value of justice so tightly, that when combined with a promise of a martyr's reward in the afterlife, they will take their own life in order to kill those who were deemed to act unjustly. In this line of thinking, all Israelis participate in the injustice against Palestinians because they stole the land in 1948, so all are guilty. While the majority of the Muslims I have talked to do not condone violence and the actions of the extremists, it has been clear in some of those conversations that there is a confusing justification that is found within the religion. Since 2000, about 1,000 Israelis have been killed, and over 9,000 injured in these types of attacks. Many Israelis are terrified to get on buses, and feel anxious in crowded places because of the rampant terrorism that took place between 2000 and 2005. This we have heard of. This made our news.

We are told that the wall is to keep the "Jihad Muslim Terrorists" from blowing up Jews. And since the wall went up the bombings have decreased by ninety-eight percent. There are two sides to every story. Husam told us the side of the story that never makes our televisions screens and newspapers. He told us that there is no justification for the violence that the extremist Palestinians responded with during the Second Intifada. He also told us that although 1,100 Israelis were killed, over 6,000 Palestinians were killed in the same length of time. And while there have been over 9,000 injuries to Israelis, there have been over 49,000 injuries to Palestinians. These are the numbers we don't hear about. These are the numbers that don't make our news.

Husam made it very clear that the wall didn't stop the bombings, but the Palestinians stopped bombing when the Intifada ceased, and the majority of the extremists and militants had been arrested. He pointed to the wall covered in graffiti to our left. "If we wanted to, we could get over that wall no problem. We do it all the time. And if we couldn't get over the wall, then we could shoot rockets over it. But we choose not to." Then he went on to explain what Palestinians see as the purpose of the wall. "The wall is there to humiliate us. The wall cuts us off from hospitals, from schools, from the water wells, and from the fertile and grazing land. The wall is there to make our lives so impossible that we will leave the country."

The more Husam spoke and the more I saw, the harder it became to process. I heard what he was saying, and I agreed. It made me want to hand someone a rock to throw. It made me angry. It made me wonder if I woke up and found myself trapped on this side of the situation, what would I do? But I can't forget the Jew whose entire family was incinerated, not because of who they weren't, but because of who they were. And that Jew survived and got on a boat and came here because the world said to. And now another group of angry people are trying to blow him up. So he builds a wall to try to protect his life, his family, and his home. The reality of the violence and hatred that both these groups of people have faced, historically and daily, is jarring. Taking in the two stories, still with the ability to go home to my America, it feels like standing in between two stacks of speakers blaring two different songs.

Our next stop was the Aida Refugee Camp. It looks nothing like the camp it began as. In 1950, the camp started with 800 displaced Palestinians. For the first seven years they lived in tents that the UN provided. Refugee camps are meant to be temporary, but the problem was these people had nowhere to go. They weren't allowed to go back to their homes, many were shot dead for trying. And if they left the country, like many did during the Al-Nakba, they would never be let back in. After seven years, the UN made shelters. They built one-room shelters for families of six, and two-room shelters for families of seven and larger. Israeli towers manned with snipers were also built. The camp has grown from a population of 800 to 7,800 Palestinians. The population has grown, but the area of the camp has remained the same: one-half square mile.

We entered into a third world as we walked the streets of the camp. I felt nervous. There is no grass, and there are no trees. All you see is concrete. With no room to expand out, they expanded up. Every building is within inches of the next, and a few narrow pathways make up a maze throughout. The community shares outdoor toilets and showers. Sixty years has passed, and for the majority of the people who live here, these conditions are all they have ever known. But they know it's wrong because in sight is a five-star Israeli hotel. Also in sight is a huge water tower painted with a massive Israeli flag. Imagine living on top of your neighbors and your neighbor's neighbors, sharing a single room with five other people and going outside to find that your water has been cut off. Maybe you have no power on this day, so it's very dark. What catches your eye? The not-too-far-off, lit water tank, full of water you can't have, painted with the flag of those who control you.

Abdelfattah, a man who lives in the camp and runs an arts and theater program for the children promoting "beautiful resistance", spoke to us about the refugee camp. There are two things he said that I will never forget. "Our every breath is controlled by the rhythm of the Israeli occupation. Our every move is controlled by the rhythm of the Israeli occupation. Every love relationship is controlled by the rhythm of the Israeli occupation. And every family is controlled by the rhythm of the Israeli occupation. But for us to respond with the practice of violence is to lose what is left of our humanity."
And he also said this. "There is absolutely no privacy in this place. We can smell our neighbor's bread baking next door. But when we go long enough without smelling any bread, we know to take them some food."

We continued to walk. I was inspired by their resilience, but that was trumped by the injustice. I couldn't look anymore. I remember watching the footsteps and shoes of the friend in front of me and feeling heavy. And when I looked up, I made eye contact with a boy sitting on some steps a few feet to my right. Before I had time to smile, he looked at me with cold eyes. And from his side he rose his hand, and in his hand was a black gun. Everything in me stopped. And I watched as he pulled the trigger of the gun pointed at my head. He shot me in the neck with a plastic bullet. Holding my neck, heart racing, I looked away and closed my eyes tight, realizing it was just a toy. I remember saying to myself out loud, "Really?" And then I said to Nick, the guy wearing the shoes I had been following, "He shot me. He shot me in the neck." And we continued walking.

On any other day in any other place having a gun pointed and fired at me would be the end of that day. I would go home. And there's a good chance someone would have to put me back together. But in that place something made it okay. As I continued to walk and my heart slowed, something told me, *"You're okay, because your moment of terror will never be as great as the terror that the people here experience day in, day out."*

We left the camp to climb up a nearby rooftop to get a perspective of the entire refugee camp and surrounding area. As I sat on the ledge of the roof, enjoying the warm blowing breeze, I could see Husam's lips moving, but I couldn't make myself move closer. I had no more space in that moment to hear and take in more. Later I would find out he was speaking about an event that happened in 1992. After some research I was astounded by what I found. In December 1992, six Israeli soldiers were murdered and a sergeant was kidnapped by the Islamic fundamentalist group Hamas. Hamas demanded that their founder and spiritual leader, Yassin be released from prison. Israel's Prime Minister Rabin did not meet the ransom, and the sergeant was killed. In response to this, a list of over 400 names was drawn up. In a covert mission, these 400 men would all be taken from their homes in the middle of the night, blindfolded and cuffed, transported over the border of Lebanon, and dropped off in the middle of nowhere on a cold mountainside in no-man's land. Among these Palestinian men were lawyers, doctors, scientists, university professors, religious leaders and businessmen. They were all said to have ties to Hamas. They had been deported to an area in the woods that they were told they wouldn't be able to leave for two years. They were given tents, cots, and meager rations of food. The

UN passed a resolution condemning Israel for what they had done and demanded the men be returned to their homes. Israel was able to hold up the process in court for over a year while the men were confined to the camp. I read a book about a Christian man named Brother Andrew who went to visit the men multiple times. After hearing their stories, he shared with the public that he believed the men he met had nothing to do with Hamas. Slowly but surely over a period of two years, the men were returned to their families, and Israel eventually released a statement that said, "Many of the men were taken by mistake."

Most tourists that have been to Israel on a tour of the Holy Land don't even realize they entered the West Bank. But they all do for a quick in and out, two-hour max, visit to Bethlehem and the Church of the Nativity. It makes sense that they wouldn't know because their buses use the settler/tourist highways and steer clear of all things Palestinian. While most get a unrealistic view of the West Bank, I felt up in arms about the view of Bethlehem and the Nativity. No fields, no stables, no inn, no manger, just a dirty, built-up city and another big-ass church. This church, like the Holy Sepulchre in the Old City, was also built by Constantine's mom, Helena. We walked through with the scores of other tourists and touched the spot where Mary was said to have delivered Jesus, and then walked over to the spot that the manger was said to have been. This time I didn't even try to be spiritual, instead I tried to take in what I was seeing and compare it to what I had previously known. I was distracted by the story that Husam shared right before we went in about the monks who run the church. The monks represent different churches and tend to disagree when it comes to everything. We were shown a ladder leaning up against a wall that apparently had been there for years, because they could not agree on who was allowed to move it. And there was a legendary, brutal fight between two monks with brooms that happened over who got to clean the floor. It's disappointing. I remember being out of water and crazy thirsty. As we left the church, Husam stopped us in the courtyard. "Look up. See all those bullet holes?" In 2002 the Israelis occupied Bethlehem to capture some Palestinian extremist militants, and the extremists fled to the church and took over 200 monks and Palestinians hostage for 39 days. That's crazy.

That night we went to a special place for dinner called The Tent. It was literally a big tent. We ate a lot of food on more little plates than could fit the table. We also smoked apple hookah. I didn't smoke much hookah, but I did partake in a couple cold beers. I figured I deserved something refreshing for getting shot at.

 **day five**

Every morning the first thing I did soon after opening my eyes was an ankle check. Even with an entire night with my feet far above my head, up on two hotel pillows and my doughnut travel pillow, I was beginning to think I was destined for butterball roly-poly stubs for life. On this day I got up extra early to go on a special mission. Before I left for Israel a friend told me to go to the Holy Sepulchre early in the morning before all the tour buses arrived. He said that it was his favorite morning of his entire trip. I convinced my friends JD and Kate, who also didn't make it into Jesus' empty tomb when we were there before, to come with me for a second attempt. More than anything, I needed JD to figure out how to get us there through the maze of streets in the Old City. We got to the Holy Sepulchre not long

 after the Muslims unlocked the front door, and there were still lots of people roaming around. Going downstairs, we found the big room with the mini-stone room inside it. We walked into the small entrance room, and a nun

61

shut the heavy door behind us. The front part that we were in was lit by candles and was the size of a round elevator. There was a tiny opening into the tomb room, no more than three feet high and the wall that surrounded it was at least a couple feet thick. It was us, the nun, and one other chubby white lady. We could see the legs of what looked like a lot of people squashed into the place we wanted to go. They were saying some sort of prayer. We'd wait in our stuffy little room until they filed out, and then it would be our turn to go in. Five minutes passed, they kept praying, and we stood quiet. Then ten minutes passed, still praying, and we decided they must be having a Catholic mass. It couldn't go too much longer, we thought after twenty minutes had gone by. At thirty minutes we were totally over it, but we had already waited so ridiculously long in this claustrophobic stone room, that clearly we couldn't give up our spot now. The nun lady started kneeling, then standing up, then kneeling, and after a few crosses of herself, we thought we our time had come. Ten minutes later, the Catholics piled out one by one, and we squeezed over to the right to make room for them. Chubby lady was just about to duck under when a monk came in and announced we needed to clear out for the next mass to come in. JD politely explained that we hadn't been in yet, and we'd just waited forty minutes for our turn. The monk didn't care. "We need to keep to the schedule. You can't go in." JD responded, "We just need thirty seconds to see our Savior's empty tomb! Thirty seconds!" At this point I'm literally shoving chubby lady through the hole, whispering, "Go lady, just go." She was too scared of the monk to disobey, and then he edged himself between us and the hole. "You need to leave." As I reluctantly backed out with the meanest look I could conjure up, I whisper-yelled, "I don't like you, monk." It was so stupid. That is the most stupid experience I have ever had. We walked all the way back to the hotel complaining, groaning, and laughing at how stupid that was.

Thankfully we were heading far away from the Old City, southeast, for the Dead Sea and Masada. My mom floated in the Dead Sea when she was my age, and said there is nothing else like it. I was excited to experience the saltiest body of water on earth for myself, and hoped this recommendation would hold up better than the last. But before we did any floating, we were going for a hike up Masada.

If the temperature at eight o'clock in the morning when we loaded the bus was any indication of the day, we were in for a scorcher. As we descended from Jerusalem into the desert and my friends chatted in pairs in the seats ahead of me, I quietly tried to convince myself to buck up. *Who cares if it is a million degrees and your legs ache like hell, buck up and hike.* When we pulled into the parking lot, the desert mountain that we were about to climb was so tall I had to get out of the bus to see the top. I could see a line of ant-sized people slogging their way up a zig-zagged path carved into a barren and brown beast of a hill.

I could also see a cable car that hovered high above the path, making its way with ease to the top. My marathon-running friends were giddy to hike. I was giddy to watch them hike as I floated far above them in the air conditioning. Historically, I'm not one to bail on physical challenges. A couple years earlier, a handful of friends and I did a three-week trek in the snow-covered Himalayas. A few days shy of the end I strained a tendon in my knee. With no road out, and no transportation lacking heart beats for thirty miles, we made crutches and I hopped for three days to the finish. I did try to rent a donkey, and I would have definitely opted for a cable car or even a zip-line had there been one. I guess the only reason I didn't bail was because there was no other option. So, it might not be the best comparison. But if it was as stifling hot in those Nepali mountains as it was on this day, I'd still be there. The point is, I did not want to hike.

Just as I was about to go public with my surrender, Jer walked over and announced, "I've got bad news. Apparently, it's so hot that they've closed the mountain to hiking up to protect from sun poisoning and heat exhaustion. So sorry guys. Looks like we have to take the cable car up." Everyone was clearly disappointed. I was doing secret somersaults in my head while trying to look sad.

Why would anyone build a cable car in the middle of the desert to get up a flat-topped mountain? There is a fascinating story behind why this rocky plateau is now considered a Jewish pilgrimage site. In the time-line of Jerusalem there was a short period in which the Jewish Maccabees took control of the city. It is said that in that time, about 100 BC, Jonathan the High Priest built a hidden settlement on top of a mountain in the middle of nowhere, just outside of the center of everything. In the 30's BC, King Herod, the crazy king obsessed with building absurdly large things, took over Masada and made it a fortress and refuge from his enemies in case of rebellion, and it seconded as his winter palace overlooking the Dead Sea.

Once we were at the top, the Sun was so incredibly harsh that it felt like it was sucking the life out of us faster that we could suck down our quickly-disappearing water. We walked around the ruins and remnants of what looked to be a small village, stopping to take cover under white canvas tarps stretched out to create shade. Climbing stairs, we stepped out onto a second-story patio of sorts with an outlook that spanned miles of desert and sea. A drawing of King Herod sprawled out in an over-sized chair on this same patio, with servants at his left and right fanning him with palm branches, caught my eye. *Where did they get the branches? There is nothing but sand as far as I can see. And I wish I was Herod.*

In 70 AD the Romans destroyed the second temple and all of Jerusalem. The Great Jewish Revolt that led up to that included the conquest of Masada by an extremist group led by a Galilean. The rebel community grew to 960 people over a span of about seven years. In 73 AD the Romans decided to take back Masada and put an end to the last rebel stronghold in Judea. The Roman Legion led a siege up the mountain with 8,000 troops. They didn't get very far very fast. There was no way up. It was a

64

most perfect and protected fortress. The troops labored for months in the evening and through the night to build a ramp of rock and sand. Looking over the west side, you can still see where they literally moved the earth by hand, hundreds of thousands of tons of dirt, to make a way to the top. As I looked down over the edge, it was easy to imagine the anxiety they must have felt as they watched the troops progress. I imagine that's what they did every day all day. I imagined this community of rebels, women, and children spending all their time watching.

And then there came a day when the ramp reached the top and the men climbed over the wall, ready to finish the battle they had been anticipating for months. Yet instead of attack, they were met by silence. What they came to do had already been done. Left for them was a pile of bodies. It was a mass suicide. The leaders of the community persuaded their people that it was better to die by their own hand than to give up their land and their freedom. I have a hard time calling it a mass suicide. It was recorded that the men drew lots to determine who would do the slaying and when there was one man left, he fell on his own sword.

Standing in full sun, thirsty and ready to go down, I looked around at the many Jewish tourists being led by their guides. How could they celebrate the heroism of a massacre of their own, by their own, for the sake of pride over a piece of land? I understand that throughout time they have always been the underdogs. They've always survived and overcome. I have incredible respect for that, but in that moment I couldn't understand what happened in Masada then and what's happening in Masada now. I just wanted down.

Before we left for a visit to the Dead Sea, I ran into the gift shop to use the bathroom. It was like most bathrooms, with stall doors that had the turn knob which would read either a green vacant or a red occupied. Naturally, I pushed open a green vacant door to be met by a squatting, small, old, Asian woman. She looked me in the eye and let out a loud and karate-chop-like "Hie-gh!". Startled, I turned and ran away. She scared me.

When we got to the Dead Sea it reminded me of a small-scale Mexican resort. One of my friends asked, "Everyone is in bathing suits here. Aren't the Muslims very modest?" The answer to that question is a sobering reminder of the division of Israel. The reason the Muslims weren't covered up was there were no Muslims. And there were no Muslims because Palestinians are not allowed in this part of the state of Israel. Many Palestinians can see this salty lake from where they live, but very few have had a chance to visit it since 1948.

The Dead Sea is at the earth's lowest elevation, 1,300 feet below sea level. It is 33.7% salt. Imagine taking a glass and filling it with one-third salt and two-thirds water. Mix it together and you have the Dead Sea. No animal can survive in it, hence the name.

Before we went down to the beach I made a second attempt to use the bathroom and change into my suit. As I walked back to the changing room after buying a huge bottle of freezing cold water, I saw my friends Carli and Jenna come out of the exit door. I went into what I thought was the entrance door to the women's changing room and was met by a hairy, naked old man. Again, I turned and ran away. I scared him.

I made my way to the actual women's bathroom saying to myself, *"Really? Twice in one day. Really?"*

The sand is so hot it burns your feet to stand on it. The water feels more like shower gel than it does water. As you get in, your feet sink down into the dark-grey sticky mud, making it next to impossible to walk. If it gets into your eyes, you're toast. It burns more than I imagine using lemon juice as eye drops would. There are no splash fights in the Dead Sea. Even if just a little water touches your lips, it's intensity is overwhelming.

66

There is no treading water in the Dead Sea. It's impossible to sink. You can literally lay on your back and raise your arms and your legs into the air at the same time. We all got into a circle, floating on our backs with all our toes touching in the middle as we held hands. We looked like a sky diving team in a mid-jump formation. After enough time in the salt we covered ourselves head to toe in the gooey mud, said to be like the fountain of youth for the skin, and then I was ready for the shade. Jer and I transitioned to wicker chairs in a little cabana next to a refreshment shack and sipped on cold beers for a good hour. Our pace had been so fast and full until this point that both Jer and I took long breaks from our own conversation. There was something precious about the silence, in suits and board shorts, with cold drinks. It was a break from the tension, a break from being peppered with new information and history, a break from trying to stuff down being absolutely overwhelmed to make room for the stories that deserved my space. When the rest of our group didn't appear like we expected, instead of going to look for them, we got a second beer.

Back at the Capitol Hotel that night, we had a free evening to walk into the old city and get dinner on our own. After a long shower to get the mud out of my ears, Sarah, Jeff, John, and I decided to go on a hunt for shawarmas. Ramadan was officially over and the streets were no longer swarming with people and vendors. To get into the old fortified city for our first four days, we walked about half a mile down along the wall to enter in through the Damascus Gate, but tonight there was a much closer gate open. Assuming it had been closed during Ramadan, we entered through it hoping to find our way and save some time. John was leading the way, confident in his sense of direction, and clearly up for a little adventure. There were very few people entering into this gate compared to the other, and my sense was that if it connected to the shops, everyone else would take this way too. I said, "I don't know if this will connect. It doesn't feel right."

"Let's just see where it takes us." John said with a boyish smile. Jeff was game, and Sarah seemed neutral. As we navigated our way through the thin maze of alleys, it quickly got dark and quiet. We were the only ones there, surrounded by rows of ancient buildings all cut from the same rock. There was dim light stretching from street lamps every hundred yards or so. It was beautiful and haunting. We were in the Muslim quarter's residential area. It was too dark and too quiet. John was on an adventure, but I was uncomfortable. We were four Americans with four hundred dollar iPhones in our pockets, along with passports and enough cash to feed a hungry family for months. We were there to stand in solidarity with the Palestinians, but they didn't know that. I know all it takes is one or two men with guns and your whole life changes. My heart was pounding, "John, we need to turn around and go back now. This isn't safe."

I could tell he didn't really want to, but he wanted me to feel safe. So, we turned around and headed back. Sarah was on my left, and we were following behind the guys. As we continued to walk, my eye was drawn to my right down another dark alley, and without wanting to, I made eye contact with a man as he stepped out from a doorway about twenty-five yards away. In his hand down by his side, I could see he had a handgun. Panic screamed through my insides. "We need to walk faster!" There was no way to know if it was a coincidence or if he'd seen us from a window or the roof. We walked fast and left through the gate a few long minutes later. If I had been by myself I would have run. My hands and voice were shaky. I could feel and hear my pulse. No one else saw the man. We had seen many men and women with guns, but they were all Israeli military. Palestinians aren't allowed to have guns.

We walked to the Damascus Gate, entered into the Old City, and walked in circles for another twenty minutes. Everything was closed. After leaving the Old City for a second time we grabbed street food at the busy square just outside the gate. This was where all the people were. Sarah and I shared a shawarma filled with meat, veggies, and tahini sauce and wrapped in a pita. We sat down at a grouping of tables facing the busy street while the boys stood and waited for their food behind us. Suddenly, there was some sort of commotion on the street. We watched in shock as we saw a man chasing another man down the street, holding a table above his head. They ran out of our sight before we saw any tables thrown. Sarah looked at me with wide eyes, "What just happened?" With eyes equally as wide I responded, "I have no idea." And then we saw the same guys all running back from where they had just come from, minus the table. We watched as they ran down the street and toward where we were sitting. These four or five guys ran right up to the tables and stopped in their tracks all within a few feet of us. One of the guys stood close with hands awkwardly behind his back. And then an Israeli Defense vehicle came from the same direction with its police lights flashing. The men were desperately trying to blend in. It was like we were in a massive time-out. I could feel the eyes of hundreds of Palestinians watching us. The once chaotic and loud square stood frozen and silent as the SUV slowly passed through. It felt as if we were in the center of a riot on pause, and everyone was watching to see what was going to happen next. Sarah and I looked at each other without a word, slowly stood up, and walked as quickly as our legs would take us, as if our lives depended on it, over to Jeff and John, just before the IDF car was out of sight. The guys had just gotten their food, and had their backs turned to all that had happened moments before. They thought we were crazy. We walked quickly back to the Capitol, getting shawarma juice all over our hands as we went. That night from my bed I heard gun shots. I was thankful this would be our last night in East Jerusalem, but anxious for the next three nights in the West Bank.

 **day six**

This day would be by far the most intense of the entire trip. It was a day of tug-of-war, and we were the rope. This was our dual-narrative day in Hebron. We would jump back and forth between the Jewish narrative and the Palestinian narrative from the day's beginning to the day's end.

Hebron is another city rich with story, and like Jerusalem, it has changed hands many times between the Jews and the Arabs over the course of history. Hebron is located in the West Bank and is racked with tension and conflict. The West Bank is the area that was allocated to the Palestinians after the 1948 War. In 1967 there was another war that lasted six days. The surrounding Arab countries of Jordan, Syria, and Egypt were defeated by Israel. Depending on who you speak to, you'll get a very different story of how and why the war started. The outcome was that Israel acquired more land from the Palestinians and took control of Jerusalem from Jordan. The West Bank shrunk. Shortly after the war ended 25,000 Palestinian houses were demolished. The West Bank was Palestinian territory under Jordanian control, but after 1967 it became occupied and under the control of the Israelis. Within the West Bank are Jewish settlements. Palestinian land and homes are bought or demolished by the Israeli government in order to create space to build highly protected Jewish communities. The building of these settlements is illegal according to international law, yet new settlements are still being built and the existing settlements continue to expand throughout the West Bank. The settlers who live in these communities are there for a handful of different reasons. The government highly subsidizes the cost to live there. Some Israelis live there because it's affordable. Many live in the settlements because they are Zionists devoted to taking back control of the entire land of Israel in order to rebuild the temple and see the coming of the Messiah. And many choose to live there in the midst of great conflict because they want the land for the State of Israel.

The settlements are all connected by a series of Israeli roads. These roads are also protected. Palestinians are not allowed to drive on them or even cross them, except at certain check points, or only if they obtain hard-to-get permits. Imagine a giant, thick spider web woven throughout your home. You are not allowed to touch it or step through it. So, now your life changes dramatically. Many of the rooms of your house are now off limits. Your mother who lives upstairs, you're no longer able to see her. And forget about getting any chores done. What can you do? Hang out in the one room without a web and be mad at the spider.

You can find Hebron in the Bible. In Genesis, Abraham bought land that contained caves from a Hittite, and it would become the burial plot for his family. This story is the first record of Jewish ownership of land in Hebron. However, Muslims also have a connection to Abraham. It's complicated. Hebron followed a very similar timeline to Jerusalem when it came to who had control. We don't know exactly when the burial place of Abraham, his sons Isaac and Jacob, and their wives was first discovered, but it was Herod who built it into a great walled shrine known today as the Cave of the Patriarchs. Later, under Islamic rule, the shrine was turned into a mosque and they built domes over the tombs of Abraham and Sarah. Eventually, the Crusaders pushed their way in and made it a church. And after they were kicked out by another Islamic army, and after a few changes, it went right back to being a mosque. The shrine/mosque/church of the "father of all nations" is considered the second holiest Jewish site behind the Western Wall, and it's also a pilgrimage site for Muslims and Christians. It was closed to non-Muslims for almost a thousand years until after the war in 1967.

What is unique about Hebron is in the early 1900's, there was a strong presence of the Jewish community, and they lived in peace among their Arab neighbors. In 1929, there was a gruesome massacre in Hebron of 67 Jews, including women and children by Arab terrorists. It was a surprise attack of neighbors killing neighbors. After the massacre the majority of the Jews left Hebron for safer ground. The relationships that existed between Arabs and Jews were replaced by division, deep-rooted hurt, and mistrust.

After 1967, the Jews returned to build what is known to many as the most violent and heavily protected settlement in the West Bank. The Cave of Patriarchs stayed under Muslim control, but was opened to the Jews as well. In 1994, there was another massacre, but this time a Jewish settler went into the mosque, killing 29 Muslims and wounding another 120. There were Israeli soldiers present who stood by and watched, holding their guns, because it was against orders to shoot a Jew even if he is harming other humans. Now the holy site is divided right down the middle by a wall to keep Jews on one side and Muslims on the other.

In 1997, the violence between the two communities had been so constant and grave that it was decided Hebron would be split into two sections, H1 and H2. Israel handed H1, about eighty-percent of Hebron, over to the Palestinian Authority and the 140,000 Palestinians that live there. H2 is under Israeli control and is inhabited by 30,000 Palestinians, and 500 Israeli settlers. There are over 1500 Israeli soldiers on duty in Hebron to protect its 500 settlers. That's easy math, three soldiers to protect each settler. There have been many murders and attacks between the two communities despite the high security. The violence from settlers against Palestinians was so great that a team of neutral observers have been brought in from other countries to walk the streets unarmed and report all unjust actions to both Israeli and Palestinian authorities and six others countries. This is Hebron.

In the morning we were dropped off in Hebron at a check point. It was as far as our Palestinian driver Issa could bring us. He would pick us back up in the same spot in early evening. The check-point was a small trailer that blocked a thin street into the center of town. I walked through the trailer to have my passport examined by multiple armed soldiers after being thoroughly searched. The corner that Issa dropped us off was part of a busy city with cars honking and shops spilling into the streets. Stepping out of the trailer onto the other side of the street was like walking into a ghost town. Years earlier, this had been the main street for the shops and markets in Hebron. Over a thousand shops were shut down with the the the division of H1 and H2. Clearly, we were in H2, lined with boarded up shop doors below and barred windows above. We walked to meet Rabbi Eliyahu, director of the Jerusalem Peacemakers. This unconventional Rabbi led and narrated our day, and when it was finished, as the sun set, he shared with us his story.

"I'm not your typical Orthodox. I'm more of a mixed bag. My father was raised in a Christian home, but embraced Eastern spiritual practices under an Indian guru. My grandfather was a minister, and he came from a long line of Protestant pastors and reverends. My mother is Jewish and

*came from a family of rabbis. My parents met in the sixties,
which made them part of the hippie revolution. Mom was
hitchhiking to a hippie commune in Northern California, Dad
picked her up, and that's how they met. I think I have flower
power in my roots. To yearn for world peace and harmony must
have seeped into my genetic code. Spending my childhood and
adolescence in Hawaii had great influence on who I would
become. As a youth, I was searching for a sense of identity.
When I was twelve there was a boy at my school in Oahu who
invited me to his bar-mitzvah. The first time I set foot in the
synagogue, I felt a deep connection and resonance. I studied for
a year and then had my own bar-mitzvah and received my name,
Eliyahu. At age 18, I came to Israel on a birthright tour and
after high school I returned to Israel for a year. After an
extended time of living as part of a kibbutz and studying
Hebrew, I was inspired to return and live in the Holy Land. I
went to college at UC Berkeley and became very involved as a
Pro-Israel Activist. It was my job to defend Israel, but it was
during that time that I came to know the people standing behind
the Pro-Palestine table. I took a class called "Palestine" on the
history of the country. I was sent in to spy on the class, but it
opened my mind to the fact that there was another story. And as
I became aware of the current oppression and injustice, I began
to question Zionism. I even became anti-Zionist for a time. It
wasn't long before I realized I was designed to work with
bridge-building projects between Jews and Arabs, first in
Berkeley and ultimately in the Holy Land.*

Eliyahu is a special man who has dedicated his life to
peacemaking, friendship building and sharing both sides of the
story to those looking in. Peace literally oozes out of this
Berkeley, hippie, rabbi, accepter-of-all guy in a Hawaiian t-shirt.
I like him instantly. With him he brought along a random
handful of tourists from an assortment of countries who signed
up for his dual-narrative tour at a hostel. After a quick greeting,
Eliyahu, a little frazzled, tells us, "We must go quickly. Stay
close and walk fast. We are already running behind and we have
so much to see." I imagined I was feeling a lot like Charlie at
the beginning of his tour of Willy Wonka's chocolate factory.

We followed Eliyahu down the street and then a sharp turn took us up many flights of steps through fields with trees. He took us into a cave surrounded by fences. It was the tomb of Jesse and Ruth. After leaving there we weaved our way up more stairs and through a tunnel of fences into a grouping of houses. We continued to walk until we stopped at a small playground. "Please take a seat here." I had no idea what was happening. I sat on a bench and then realized we were in the settlement. The settlement. The settlement my friends and I had been talking about for months. The most violent settlement in the West Bank where the settlers attack the Palestinians while the soldiers stand by and watch. We were supposed to sit down with its leader, David Wilder, but he had taken a last-minute vacation with his family and cancelled. Instead, a small woman dragged a chair out of a very little house in the courtyard we were sitting, with one hand while holding some papers and a book tightly in the other. She sat uncomfortably in her chair and nervously faced us. As she spoke her voice was frail and quiet, and we all leaned in to best listen. This is her story.

My name is Tsipi, but that is not my real name. My real name is Sarah Ticovah; this is the name of my grandmother. And I'd like to tell you about my grandmother, and her experience in Hebron. In 1929, her sister Leah and her sister's husband, Yakov, lived in Hebron and had a baby. Yakov had to go to Jerusalem, so her two sisters, one of which was my grandmother, came to stay with her. That same day, the Arabs had the pogrom and attacked a group of Jews in Jerusalem. At that time in Hebron, unlike Jerusalem, there was a very good relationship between the Arabs and the Jews here. They lived like a big family. The surrounding area wanted to send people and weapons to defend the Jews in Hebron from the Arabs. But the Jews in Hebron said it wasn't necessary because

we had such great relationships with the Arabs that no one would attack us. It came out that it was the opposite. Good friends changed their mind even though at that time there was no State of Israel or occupation. They attacked the people in a terrible way. But my grandmother had a miracle, and this is why I can talk to you today. The neighbor, Dan Slone, was the manager of the bank of Hebron. He called the people to come and hide in his house. When he heard the Arabs were coming to kill the Jews he said, "If you come to my house nothing will happen. I am friend to many Arabs and have a very good position with them. They won't harm us."

Dan Slone's father went next door to Leah and said, "Come to my house." She said, "No, I have a new baby, and if there is a crowd he might get sick. So, Dan Slone's father said he would stay with them and the baby at Leah's house. They all hid, in a store room. Then suddenly my Aunt Leah said to my grandmother, "Where you are standing is not safe!" And she pushed her to the other side of the store room. And just minutes later, an Arab threw a large rock through the window and it fell in the same place where my mother was standing. Leah says she heard the screaming of the children in Dan Slone's house. The Arabs came and killed everyone in their home except one who survived. They were killed by their friends. Dan, his wife, his children, and all who he tried to protect were killed by their neighbors. This is my family's story of 1929.

Many years later and 14 years ago, Prime Minister of Israel, Netanyahu gave control of Hebron to the Arabs. And 97% of Hebron became closed to the Jews. I can no longer go to the house of my Aunt Leah, next door to the Slone's house.

Netanyahu meant the division to be a peace process. The Arabs got what they wanted, so they should have been nice to the Jews. But they kept asking for more. This happened at a special time of the year when by tradition Jews come to the caves to pray. At the same time a young couple with little money and no family wanted to get married. My father volunteered to help them with the wedding, and I have this picture of them all dancing together at the reception. My father was a quiet and calm Rabbi who devoted his life to studying the Torah. Even the Arabs said hello to him because they knew and respected him as a kind man and rabbi. We are sitting in front of what was my family's home. An Arab terrorist came through the back window of the house just a few hours after this picture was taken at the wedding. My father was in his pajamas, he went to sleep, and my mother who was in the other room heard terrible screaming. She said she had never heard my father scream in her life. My mother said even when I was a child and we did something bad, she used to tell him, "Yell at them!" But he never did.

The Arab stabbed him, but he was able to run into the other room to where my mother was, and then the Arab stabbed him again in the heart. There was nothing she could do to help him. The Arab lit a molotov cocktail explosive and threw it in the house. When the house started to burn my mother started to scream, and the Arab ran away leaving through the same window. A neighbor came and extinguished the fire before the entire house burned to the ground. This is my family's story in Hebron.

My mother said it was very hard for her to stay after she saw what they did to my father. But she also said she couldn't leave this place because this is what the terrorists wanted. So, she called the people of Hebron and asked them to make a Yeshiva in the same room that my father was killed. They made the room a little bigger, and still today the students study the Torah in that same spot. This is often the Jewish response to terror attacks. We go to the same spot, and we build something bigger to say that we are still here. After my mother's petition, it was a government decision to allow the caravans that we lived in to be replaced by permanent houses in response to my father's death.

I have papers from 200 years ago in this book to show that the Jewish community bought this land. When the British were here, they checked the land, and declared it an archaeological dig because this area is of Abraham, Isaac, and King David. But when they started the building for the Yeshivas 14 years ago, they discovered the walls of an old city from 4500 years ago and steps to a house with four rooms. Inside one of the rooms they found artifacts, one being a pitcher with a carving of a bird with Hebrew writing, the language of the Jews, on the handle that said "To the king of Hebron". I believe that because of my father's death we have this proof that the Jewish community has

78

*a very strong connection to this place because we have been in
this spot for centuries.*

*Twelve years ago, two years after my father's death, his
murderer was freed in a prisoner exchange. If you asked me if I
have any connections to the Arabs in Hebron now, the answer is,
I have a feeling they would do to me what they did to my father,
so no connection. But I feel safe here. We have a normal life
here. There are 90 families in our community who feel the same.
This is our place, we have no other place.*

The picture I had of the violent settler was shattered from the
moment Tsipi whispered out her first words. This was the first
I'd heard about the massacre in 1929. From there Eliyahu led us
to a small museum depicting the events of the massacre. It was
an almost silent walk as we all attempted to shuffle around
everything we had learned about the settlers prior to this day to
make room for Tsipi. There was a piece of me that wanted to
jump ship and switch sides. I know we specifically came to not
take sides. But if I'm honest, my experiences with Palestinians
had not been overwhelmingly positive so far. I knew better, but
it was confusing to say the least. The museum consisted of four
small rooms of gruesome pictures and articles retelling the story
of that day in 1929. Eliyahu told us that the one story that was
missing from the museum was the one of the survivors. The
many Jews who survived the massacre survived because their
Arab neighbors took them in, protected them, and hid them.
Every story has two sides.

Next, we left the settlement and walked to the Jewish side of the
Cave of Patriarchs. After squeezing through heavy security, we
made our way to see the tombs of Abraham and Sarah. We
passed through quickly feeling the palpable tension. The cave is
separated by a temporary plywood divider- Jews on one side,
Arabs on the other. The sounds of the contrasting prayers, the
sight of such a heavy military presence, and the knowledge of
the massacre that took place in this spot was all unnerving. It
was enough to quicken my pace and I felt relief when Eliyahu
corralled us toward the exit. It was time for a special traditional
meal in the Palestinian home of Rebhi and his family in H1.
Eliyahu partnered with Rebhi for these tours to give us an inside

look into the culture while providing Rebhi with a little extra income. Before we began, there was a blessing, like no other blessing I have ever experienced. First Rebhi offered a Muslim blessing in Arabic, then Eliyahu gave a Jewish blessing in Hebrew, and then Jon said a Christian prayer in English. Next, we were escorted upstairs to a small room with a large rug stretched across its floor, and a score of small plates piled high with different foods for us. We lined the walls after taking our shoes off and sat knee to knee Indian style. Rebhi's hospitality was incredible; he, his wife, and their children came with tray after tray of drinks, soups, and entire chickens. For dessert we were served a wonderful strong tea and fancy, little cookies. I ate about a third of the tray of those delicious cookies, you don't see too much dessert in Israel. With empty coffee cups and full bellies Rebhi sent us on our way.

Still in H1, we were led off the street and down a flight of stairs into a basement meeting room. We had no idea what was happening. Sitting down in the chairs set out for us, we were given a powerpoint presentation by a tall and well-spoken Palestinian man by the name of Walid. He shared with us what life is really like in H1 and H2 for the Palestinians under Israeli occupation. He shared that within the one-square kilometer of Hebron's center, there are over one hundred closures of streets, entrances, and exits that make it an impossible maze for its people. What used to be a two-minute walk can easily turn into twelve kilometer. Shops have been forced to close, homes vacated, and any Palestinian transportation in Hebron is prohibited. They have to carry everything in from the outside.

Walid's mission is to resist non-violently by making Hebron beautiful. His organization does renovation projects of dilapidated buildings to send the message, "We love this place. And we're not leaving."

I liked Walid. As we left, I shook his hand and said, "I respect you." He held my hand tight, stopped shaking it, but didn't let go, and said, "I know you do. I can see it in your eyes. Thank you."

Next we were met by Adeeb. He was young, nervous, and brand new to tour guiding. Eliyahu had taken him under his wing, plus we needed a Palestinian tour guide for this part of our tour. To go into the Ihibrimi Mosque, Eliyahu had to go undercover stuffing his braided sideburns under his hat and pretending to be an American tourist like the rest of us. I had never been in a mosque before. After multiple security checks, we took our shoes off and the girls were all given full-length robes with hoods to wear. We entered a huge room with high ceilings and tall, supporting pillars throughout. The rugs that spanned the entire mosque felt soft under my feet. We spread out. This was the place of the massacre in 1994 that killed 29 people and wounded many; it is also a place that Muslims pilgrimage to from all over the world. Leaning my back against a pillar, I watched as a man prayed prostrate on the floor a few feet away from me. Then a few of the other tourists that came with Eliyahu walked by speaking loudly and taking pictures. The praying man looked at them, clearly distracted, and then he looked at me. I tried to say I was sorry with a submissive nod and dropped my eyes to the floor. I shouldn't have been there. Who knows how far this man had come to worship, but he came to worship. I imagine he felt the same frustration I felt with the tourists in the Holy Sepulchre. I felt like I was stealing his experience in order to try and widen mine. I waited for the others in the room with all the shoes.

Adeeb did his best to relay a lot of information, much of which we had already heard, and many things we hadn't. He spoke as if his life depended on it, trying to squeeze as many words as he possibly could into each breath. I liked him. There was another lady on our tour who came from the hostel that I did not. She was a Jew who had come from Italy, who had no idea what this tour was when she signed up for it. At the beginning I heard her whisper, "This is all lies." But she had no choice but to stick with us because it wasn't safe for her to veer off. As Adeeb spoke about the massacre in the mosque, I could see her shaking her head, and tutt-ing to herself. And then she yelled out, "And how many Jews have you killed?" I couldn't believe it. I wanted to punch her, but then I realized we were on a peacemaking tour, so I gave her a nasty look instead. The hatred is not just found among the extremists, it's widespread.

Next we walked to the souk. Years ago, Hebron's souk was one of the busiest street markets in all of Palestine. This market had everything, but it was especially known for its artisan fine goods and olive wood carvings. Generations of tradesmen made their living and fed their family by working in the Hebron souk. Today you will find more closed stalls than open ones and a cage over top. The souk represents a turf war. Down the main street, Israel owns the top level of all the buildings, and the Palestinians still own the bottom level shops. In this case, H2 literally hovers above H1. Out of all the places I had been, I felt the least safe in the small and clogged alleyway lined in shops. Not far above our heads was a fence that caged in the souk. The fence was put in to protect the Palestinians from rocks, bricks, and the garbage that the settlers often throw down on them from above. The sun was out in all its strength, yet it felt cold and dark as we made our way through the market. The sky was blocked out by garbage, rocks, and cinderblocks. The hate was tangible.

Westerners don't often visit Hebron, and the ones that do don't come to the souk. We were a magnet to street sellers with all sorts of trinkets for us to buy. Most were respectful enough to take our third or fourth no for an answer, but there was one man who was not going to leave us alone until we gave in to him. All he had was a handful of bracelets, and he shoved them in our faces to convince us to give him money. There was something a little off about him. He was in his thirties, but stood slightly hunched over. He had yellow teeth, and an orange belt cinched around his waist to keep his pants up. I have walked through quite a few third-world, claustrophobic markets, and I can hold my own when it comes to pushy street vendors and panhandlers. But this man was relentless, and getting uncomfortably close. I had said no thank you at least ten times over the course of a half hour and each time he got more touchy and sketchy. And then I saw him corner two of the girls from our group. I yelled to get the attention of one of their husbands, but it was too loud in the souk for him to hear. As I maneuvered my way through the crowd to the girls, I could feel my blood pressure rising; I was angry. *How dare he? He has no right.* And just before I broke in to save the day and fight him if I had to, Eliyahu got there before me. He put his arm around him and said, "We love you. But we aren't going to buy your bracelets today, friend." And the man walked away.

Eliyahu was teaching me peace. It was that moment I realized how easy it is to act in anger and how hard it is to be a person of peace. In order to truly be about peace, we have to re-wire our insides and change the way we think.

In front of a stall with beautiful rugs hanging from its ceiling stood a small grey-haired man with sad eyes and a kind smile. He told us his story. His father owned this stall, and his father's father had owned it before him. The Israelis tried to buy him out, but he refuses to leave. He pointed to a small rug hanging from the cage overhead. It was covered in what looked like bleach spots. "Last year, in this spot, a settler standing on the roof above, poured a bucket of chlorine down on my son to burn

and blind him. But they did not succeed, he's had surgery and can see. My son will take over from me when I'm gone. We are not leaving. This is our home." With tears hiding beneath my sunglasses, I held his hand for longer than comfortable, and again said, "I respect you."

As we continued to walk from stall to stall, it was impossible not to feel the weight of the stories of the people who spend their days living in this tension, living in fear of what could come from above, yet living in absolute conviction and defiance for the sake of their history and home. I grew up in Florida. I didn't like it because it was flat, bland, and sticky hot. So, I moved 3,000 miles away from my family to the other side of the country for something better. As we continued to move through the souk, I had a hard time sorting out what was more ridiculous, persevering through your family being terrorized or leaving your family.

Adeeb led us down a small alley and up a tight circling staircase of stone steps to the unfinished roof of a Palestinian house. The man with the bracelets was back. He blocked my way, and when I was able to elbow my way by, he tried to follow us up the stairs. Two of the guys who lived at the house grabbed him, shoved him back, and yelled at him to leave. It was clear that they knew who he was, and he was not liked among them either. Relieved, I climbed the stairs to stand on the small open roof that overlooked all of Hebron, and the owner of the house, a man named Nidal, shared with us his story. His family has lived in this small home in the center of Hebron for generations. The stone house has three stories, two small bedrooms, and a kitchen. The Israelis offered Nidal two million dollars for his home and offered to cover all costs for his family to immigrate out of the country. "We could have had lived anywhere as kings. We could have had freedom without occupation. But we said no. Because this is our home. We live in hope of the day that we will have freedom without occupation here. If we were to sell, we would be betraying the community and all Palestinians. We would be traitors, no better than the settlers themselves."

As I carefully descended the uneven steps down from the roof and peered into the dark, furniture-less bedrooms, it was nearly impossible to wrap my head around a two million dollar offer just to get rid of one family. Our tour was over. I said goodbye to Adeeb, and we made our way out of the market to meet our bus driver. And then from behind me I felt someone grab my arm. "Bracelet, you buy." I knew I wanted to respond in peace, but putting my arm around this man was not appropriate. I wanted to help him.
"How much money have you made from our group in the last two hours?"
"Nothing, not one shekel."
"That is because you are making us uncomfortable. You are scaring us. If you step back a little, smile, and ask nicely tourists might buy from you."

He took a big step back, and smiled showing all his teeth and the ones that were missing. I thought to myself, *It's working. Maybe I'm helping him.* And then he stepped right back in, still with a forced smile, and said, "Now, you buy!"
"I'm sorry. I cannot buy today. You have already made me feel too uncomfortable. Maybe next time. I hope you are able to sell some next time."
And then I watched this man standing in front of me snap. I saw rage in his eyes. I couldn't move a muscle or make a sound. He took another step forward and leaned in until his face was within inches of mine. With a clenched jaw, and veins emerging from his forehead, he put his finger to my chest and said, "If you come back here tomorrow, I will kill you. I will kill you like I would a settler." And then he turned and walked away. It took me a second to be able to move my feet. My hands were shaking. My friend Derek saw everything. He came over and hugged me, "It happened so fast. I was on my way to punch him in the face when he walked away. I'm sorry that happened to you."
It was everything I could do to get the words out, "Will you watch for him? Don't let anything happen to me."

85

We had to wait for nearly an hour in the square for our bus. I sat sandwiched between Derek and Jer until we left that place. He could have had a knife, or he could have had a gun. I longed for the safety and stability of home.

When we got on the bus, I thought we were heading to Bethlehem back to our new hotel, but apparently we had one more stop. Eliyahu had joined us and wanted to take us to an excellent place to watch the sunset. I was ready for the day to be over, but the sun hadn't set yet. We drove for forty-five minutes east until we climbed thousands of feet in altitude to the top of a range. I always sat in the very back of the bus, which meant most of the time I didn't hear much about where we were going from the front. But this time I moved closer to listen to Eliyahu. I was fascinated by him. He was taking us to another settlement. I couldn't believe it. This had been one of the longest and most emotionally intense days of my life, and now we were going to another settlement. We were going to Tekoa; a Jewish settlement that sat on the top of a big hill. Next to it was another big hill that was home to the Palestinian village Tacia. In the beginning the settlement had good relations with the village, and they decided to do a combination school together. This is unheard of. It was a slow start, but it was growing. And then in 2001, two Israeli boys from Tekoa were murdered. The school was shut down. Later a pregnant woman from Tacia was shot in the stomach in retaliation. I wanted to stay in the bus.

We drove into the settlement on a bumpy, dirt road, and on either side of us were trailer homes. I expected it to be much different. There were no luxurious homes, no soldiers standing guard, and no concrete walls or check points to get in. Issa stopped the bus and we all filed out. What I saw next didn't feel real; it didn't line up with anything I knew or believed. The sun was within twenty minutes of setting, it was that special light that makes everything glow and look twice as beautiful as it did an hour before. We walked towards a small field of vibrant green grass lined with a few green trees that had a jungle gym and swing set in its center. As I stepped on the grass, it felt so soft and fresh compared to the dirt and concrete we had been walking on all day. On the same grass that I was now standing were a dozen young families spread out on blankets and flying kites in the cool breeze that filled the air. It was the first cool anything I had felt since stepping into the country. For the first time, the air wasn't heavy with tension, it was full of children's laughter. As we walked through the center of this make-shift park, I felt like an intruder, until I looked to my right and a beautiful woman wearing a deep-red knitted hat, sitting on a patch-work quilt with a baby in her lap, gave me the warmest smile ever and mouthed "hello" as she waved with her free hand. These people were all beautiful and happy and flying kites. It felt more like a hippy colony than it did a settlement. They weren't pouring chlorine in people's eyes. They were flying kites with their babies, and welcoming us into their little paradise.

We got to the end of the park and stepped off the grass back on to the dirt and walked towards a grouping of rocks. And there it was. A vast desert wilderness that stretched as far as the eye could see. This was the same wilderness that the Israelites wandered for forty years, the same wilderness that John the Baptist lived in and ate bugs from, and the same wilderness that Jesus spent forty days in before he began his ministry. It was like looking into the Holy Land's Grand Canyon at sunset. It was breathtaking. It was absolutely... there are no words for this moment.

For twenty minutes we spread out, we sat down, and we looked out. Everyone cried. Everyone prayed to God of this wilderness. No doubt everyone asked for peace.

And when we were ready, we stepped back on to the grass, took off our shoes, sat in a circle, and did our best to talk about the day. Eliyahu shared with us his story. And as he shared, a little boy, no more than two, in a grey tank-top and a head of wild, light-brown curls came over and infiltrated our circle to try and give Derek a cracker.

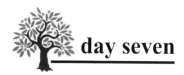 **day seven**

This morning we woke up in Bethlehem. Before breakfast I
went downstairs to the hotel lobby and hid out on one of the
many leather love seats to write an email. I was still shaken
from the day before and found myself longing for home like
never before. I wrote an emotional email to one of my
roommates telling her that I didn't feel safe, and I wanted to
come home. I wan't going to come home because I knew what
we were doing was important and special, but that didn't change
the fact that I was scared. For some reason I was the one that
kept being in the wrong place at the wrong time. No one came
into this trip with the baggage that I did, and no one else was
getting their lives threatened, shot at with plastic guns, and
finding themselves in the middle of feuds and fights. It felt like
my friends all had a false sense of security among the
Palestinians because we were there to support them. It felt like
we were walking a very dangerous line, and this morning I felt
anxious about what lay in store for us. The constant tension and
conflict had taken its toll.

At breakfast we took sometime to check in with each other. I
shared that I felt like the ground was giving way beneath me,
and no matter how hard I tried to get my footing, with every new
story, again I didn't know where to stand. I wasn't the only one
who was feeling overwhelmed. I remember JD saying, "It feels
like we haven't stopped since we got here. I just need a couple
hours by myself to try and sort the mess of emotions and
information in my head out." We were a sad and exhausted crew

that morning. And on top of it all, more than anything, I needed coffee. Not instant, nasty, pretend coffee, but a good cup of coffee.

We loaded the bus to go to the Tent of Nations. As usual, I didn't know what that was. Issa announced, "This is as far as I can take you. The road is blocked. Walk down this dirt road and you will turn right to get there. Very easy."

We walked and walked. Then we were lost. Jon said as he pointed, "I don't want to be a party pooper, but what if it's that hill way over there?" Jer ran on ahead for a few minutes. Coming back, "Nothing." We walked back the direction we came from, knowing that Issa was gone. And then we heard whistling from above. Looking up there was an old man waving his arms and motioning to us to keep walking. Further down he opened a gate and let us in. He didn't speak English. He welcomed us, "Salam." We responded to him, "Shokran." I'm terrible at remembering foreign words unless I connect them to English words. To say thank you in Arabic sounds like, "shoe-crayon", but you say crayon with an English accent. Works every time. He led us in, and within a few feet of the gate he was picking figs off a tree for all of us to try. They were drip-down-your-chin juicy and super sweet. I ate five. Next, we met Daoud. He shook all our hands and led us into a cool cave with walls covered in murals, and a long table surrounded by chairs in its center. We sat down around the table and Daoud shared with us his story.

*My name is Daoud,
and Daoud is David. I
was born in
Bethlehem, and I
finished my schooling
in 1989. It was during
that time of the First
Intifada, the
Palestinian uprising
against the
occupation, that the
Israelis closed the
schools because they
said the schools are
where the people come
together to organize themselves politically. So, we lost a
generation of young people who did nothing for three years. I
went to Austria and attended a Bible school there. When I came
back in 1991, the University of Bethlehem was reopened, so I
studied business there with a major in accounting and continued
my studies in tourism. Tourism is important here; around three
million tourists come each year to visit the Holy Land. And most
of them are Christian tourists. These tourists aren't interested in
meeting the people, or at least they don't take the time for that.
When we talk about Christian tourists, they are supposed to be
walking where Jesus walked, but they end up driving where
Jesus walked. So, no time to meet the people. And that is why
many people come and go without knowing what is going on
here. Also, many Christians don't know that there are
Christians among the Palestinians. When I was studying abroad
and speaking at churches, the first question was often "How did
you become a Christian? When did your family convert?" The
answer- 2,000 years ago. We were existing here from the
beginning.*

*We are working on a project here called the Tent of Nations.
And of course, this project is totally affected by the political
situation. Our first problem is that we are living under
occupation. And now most of the Palestinian territories are
controlled by Israel. In the peace agreement of 1993-95, the
Israeli's divided the West Bank into three zones. You came
today from Bethlehem, which is Area A, under control of the*

Palestinians. Area A are the cities. Area B are the villages, under civil control of the Palestinians, but under the military control of the Israelis. And Area C, where we are here, is under total Israeli control, which means we control nothing. Area C makes up about 70% of the West Bank, and it is in that area that the Israelis are trying everyday to build new settlements. We are in the center of five Israeli settlements.

The second problem is the roads that connect the settlements together. And the third problem is the wall that is being built on Palestinian ground. It is separating Palestinians from Palestinians, and Palestinians from their own land. Now we are part of this reality. Our piece of land was bought by my grandfather in 1916 during the Ottoman period. My grandfather was either a crazy man or a man with a vision. The first thing he did was register the land. This was unusual at that time, because many Palestinians at that time refused to register their land in order to avoid paying property taxes to their occupiers. But he always did it according to the law, and registered, and so we have papers from the Ottomans, the British, the Jordanians, and the Israelis. The second thing he did was move from Bethlehem to live on the property here in a cave, which was also unusual. Most farmers only lived on their land during harvest, and for the rest of the year they would work the land by day and return to their home at night. He did it this way because he wanted his children to grow up here. And this is exactly what happened. After my grandparents died, my father and uncle took over, and continued to farm the land living in our caves until they passed away. My father died in 1976 and he left my mother with nine children, the oldest being twenty years old and the youngest three years old. We continued as children to farm the land, but the situation changed for us in 1991 when we heard that the Israelis declared the whole area, including our farm, as state land in order to confiscate it. They wanted to take the land to build another settlement. But we have papers. So, we challenged them in the military court. We went to the court and presented the papers, and the Israelis were shocked to see documents. Because of our location, they started to make it difficult for us to prove ownership. We have been in court since 1991; 21 years of legal battle in front of the military court, and now 8 years in front of the high court. This has given us a financial burden of $150,000. One of their tactics is to place

92

obstacles in our way. For example, they want a new land survey, or proof of a new type of document, or telling us our lawyers are not recognized in front of the Supreme Court, demanding we hire new lawyers. But we are still in court, and we are the only case that is still in court since 1991. This means we have a strong case, but it is also full of frustration for us. It was their strategy to take the land, but it didn't happen because as you see, we are still here. The land we are talking about is 3,000 feet above sea level and only one hundred acres. Next, they tried with physical pressure to force us to give up and leave. We faced attacks by the Israeli settlers who came to our farm cutting down our trees, destroying our water tank, and threatening us with guns. They tried between 1991-2002 three times to build a road on our property in order to establish a settlement. We managed to stop those constructions by court. And then in 2002 they returned with big machines and started cutting the ground. We went back to the court and managed to stop them legally, again which made the settlers very angry. In retaliation they came back to our property and cut down 250 olive trees. The olive tree is a symbol of hope for peace and justice. We were very frustrated. Three weeks later, we received an email from the European Jews for Just Peace in Palestine. This Jewish group from England sponsored our farm with 250 new olive trees and then flew over to plant them. For us it was a very positive experience that made us feel like we were not alone in this struggle. With physical pressure we did not give up. We are still here and have many stories to tell.

Next, they tried to buy the land from us. They made offers of a lot of money, and the last time in 2002 they offered us a blank check, saying, "Just write down how many millions of US dollars you want for this land. And wherever you want to go, we can help you to get to any place in the world." But our answer simply was, "Our land is our mother, and our mother is not for sale." Now they are trying new strategy, which is to isolate us. Our road has been blocked since 2001. You passed by the wall coming from Bethlehem. When that wall is completed this land will be on the Israeli side, which means it won't be easy to cross back into Bethlehem. And I'm not just talking about ourselves here, but 20,000 Palestinians who will be cut off and forced to have to pass through checkpoints to get back into Bethlehem. They will be forced to leave the area. In the villages down the *hill, there are about 200 teachers that teach in Bethlehem. With the wall, they will be unable to get into Bethlehem in the thirty minutes it takes today. It could take up to five hours with the check points. This means they cannot keep their jobs unless they move into the city. This is what the Israelis want because the cities are surrounded with walls and gates like prisons, so at any time the Israelis can lock down the gates and contain up to 80,000 people at one time. The third thing we are facing on the ground here is that we are not allowed to have running water, electricity, or building permits. They are trying to make it difficult in order to force us to give up and leave. We are surrounded by settlements which by international law are considered illegal. They are illegal outposts that are built without legal permits from the Israeli government. Two years ago we received nine demolition orders for nine structures we built without a permit. Among them were tents to give shade to the animals. Three months ago we received cultivation stop orders, saying we can not grow in certain areas of our farm, because it is state land. Last May we received a demolition order for our cistern, and a week ago we received a demolition order for a tent. The tents aren't permanent, we only use them in the summers to provide shade. If we do want to build any structures, including tents, we have to apply for a building permit, and each permit we have to pay around $1,500. After forty days we will receive a letter telling us that the application is denied with no explanation of why.*

I asked an Israeli officer, "Are we all under the law here?" He said, "Yes. You cannot build without a permit." And I said," I understand. I accept this. But why don't you go to my neighbors and also give them demolition orders, not for their tents, but their houses?" He said, "This is not your business." It is not as he said, we are not all under the law.

This situation is forcing the Palestinians to act in the three different ways. The first is a violent way. Whether people believe in violence or not, when you push people to their core into the corner, it is a normal human reaction to respond in a violent way. The question is what are we achieving with reacting with violence, except more violence. All we are doing is making more enemies and more hate. Nothing can be changed through violence. The second option is to sit down and

94

cry, and be a victim, and blame the other. The victim mentality is very dangerous, because you always blame the other, even for your own mistakes. We are waiting for a savior, someone to come in and make a change for us. The third option is to run away and immigrate. And who is immigrating? The best educated Palestinians; they don't see any future here for themselves and their children. In our case, we have said we will never act in violence. We do not believe in violence. We believe in justice. Sooner or later justice will rise again. We do not hate, we believe we are all created in the image of God, and refuse to hate each other. And we refuse to be victims. We are staying here. We are not giving up. We are not passive. We want to face the situation in a different way. The three options are not good for us, so we created another way of action by saying we refuse to be enemies. This is our message. It is easy to say, but very hard to live out on the ground. We don't like others' actions against us, but we refuse to hate them as people. With this way of action, we wanted to overcome hatred with love, darkness not with more darkness, but with light. We want to change our situation with small steps to prove to people that it is possible. We created the Tent of Nations here with that slogan, "We refuse to be enemies." Our goal is to invest our frustration constructively. Because all frustration is energy. It can come out in a negative way, but we are trying with what we are doing here to channel into a positive way.

Not long ago I was driving my wife and children back from an outing to the city in our orange VW van. We were not far from here on the dirt road when we were stopped by two Israeli soldiers. The soldiers came to my window and told us we all needed to get out of the van so they could search it. When I told them that my three children were sleeping in the back, and we lived just down the

road, they said they didn't care. Again, I said if the children wake up and see you standing here with your guns they will be terrified. Please let us go home. They forced us to get out of the van. As I woke my children up, I decided to speak in English so the soldiers could understand. I said, "These men have guns, but they won't hurt you. They are very friendly." After the soldiers searched the van, one of the men pulled me aside. "I'm sorry for what we did to you and your family tonight. It wasn't right."

That night I was very frustrated, but I chose to respond in love. I spoke of the soldiers to my children as friendly humans and then one of them lived into what I had described them to be. Whenever soldiers come to drop off demolition orders I always invite them in for a cup of tea and a tour of the property. There was one soldier that came in with demolition orders, but stayed and let me show him around. After he left through the gate he walked a few feet and then came back. "I'm sorry for what is happening here. It doesn't seem right."

Our second goal is to open our farm to people from different cultures, nations, and religions to come together, and build bridges of understanding, reconciliation, and peace, especially to the Israelis. We want them to come here, because often the only picture that exists in our minds of the other is as the enemy. I know them as the radical soldier and settler, and they know me as the radical Palestinian. But when people come and see what it is we are doing here, it starts to raise questions. When we have Israelis, we don't talk about peace because you can't have peace while under occupation. But instead we say, meet the other, not as an enemy but as a human. We might disagree on many things, but it does not matter if we agree or disagree, it matters that we at least listen *to each other. This is the way of building a bridge of understanding. We believe peace is like a marathon. You cannot get it through a handshake. It is a process. You need to go through the process of understanding and the process of reconciliation. We need to look at ourselves first. If I don't have peace in my own heart, then I cannot give peace to others. As we began to develop, the challenge was how to develop without water, electricity, or building permits. For water, we are totally dependent on rain water, which we collect in cisterns. It's not much, but it is enough for the irrigation of our crops. For electricity, we managed with the help of a German non-profit to install solar panels. With the buildings, since we are not allowed to build above ground, we've decided to build below. We have seven renovated caves. We go to these great lengths to show people that things are possible.*

After we developed the infrastructure we began to invite people to come and visit and participate in projects on the land. We do children's summer camps for fifty children at a time, both Christian and Muslims. Our hope is to educate, motivate and inspire them to live in a different way. At the end of camp we invite all the parents for a festival where we share with the families the same values. The theme of the last camp was "With heart and hand we change the land."

Last year more than 5,000 people came to visit. And we hope to double that this year. For us it is not enough for people to come to the Holy Land just to visit the sites, we want them to also meet the people.

We are working to build wind turbines for electricity, and now we have composting toilets built by an Ex-Israeli settler. After a friend brought him to visit, his eyes were opened, and he left his settlement, and became involved in a group of Israelis pursuing peace. On his birthday he came back to us and built us a composting toilet. We are not changing thousands of lives, but we are changing lives one person at a time. And these are the stories that give us the encouragement and hope to continue.

Next, Daoud took us on tour of his family's one-hundred acre farm. He proudly showed us many beautiful murals painted by the children and the new olive trees. He led us to the highest spot on his property where you could see the five settlements that surrounded us. He told more stories of small victories and hope. And when we asked Daoud, "Why do you choose to live this way?", he quickly and confidently answered, "This is the way of Jesus. If I truly believe in Jesus, then there is no other option."

Before we left, we sat at a picnic table and drank tea with Daoud. I squeezed in next to him after rehearsing my words in my head and said, "Before I came here and met you I felt like the ground was crumbling beneath my feet. Everyone I have spoken with so far speaks of things that I have compassion for and want to support them in. But then at some point it is as if every person on both sides has been trying to convince me that they were the bigger victim, and some sort of justification of hate for the other would seep in to our conversation. That I cannot support and again I would lose my footing. But you, Daoud, you've given me something to stand on. There are no holes in what you speak of. You are living the way of Jesus that I have taught about many times, but you are actually teaching me what it looks like to do it."

We left the Tent of Nations a different group than we came. We were hopeful and inspired. There is peace that is being achieved in the midst of this conflict. It might be small and slow but it's real.

When we came back to the hotel, we were given what JD had asked for: a few hours of downtime. I walked down the main drag to a restaurant for tourists that sold pizza and coffee. Caffeinated, rested, and fed, I was becoming human again.

Milad

At dusk we loaded back into the bus and headed to Bethany to meet Milad and Manar who run the House of Hope. The next part of our trip was going to be working with the Palestinian children who are part of this after-school program. Milad looks like an Indian movie star and his wife has red hair and the fair skin of an Irish woman. They are both Palestinian Christians. After entering the building we were given a warm welcome by Milad and Minar and their staff. There were chairs set out in one of the classrooms for us. A big handful of children piled in the room, we sat down in the rows of chairs, and Milad shared his story. He faced us straddling his chair, facing backwards. Before long he got very intense and impassioned as he spoke, stretching his long arms out and bracing his hands to show his frustration. He reminded me of an even more intense version of Adeeb in Hebron, speaking to us as if we were the only chance at the truth of their injustice getting out to the world. Again, I had compassion for his experience, but I didn't know what to do with his anger. I remember him saying very loudly, "They rape us with their occupation!" He spoke for a very long time about the occupation and the injustice. By the end, many of us were wondering what we had gotten into. But then Milad took a step back and apologized. "I am very sorry for being so intense. This has been a very frustrating and hard year for my family. We have been so excited for you to come. You bring us hope and encouragement. Now we will go downstairs for a dance party." And that's what we did. More of the staff and kids showed up, a couple guys played hand drums, there was singing in Arabic, and we danced. We all danced on the patio under the stars for hours. We might not have known the words or the moves, but whether Arab or American, we were all equally sweaty and swept into the impromptu fun.

 **day eight**

In a failed search for my morning cappuccino in a culture that doesn't open its doors for business before eleven o'clock in the morning, I poked my head in the only open little corner store in Bethlehem.

"What do you need?" inquired the gray-haired shop keeper.

"Coffee."

"Sit. I'll make."

Knowing he was probably offering the same instant coffee as our hotel, I tried to kindly decline, but found myself sitting instead. He disappeared back into his house through the back of the shop, and minutes later came back with two small cups of Turkish coffee. I asked, "How much?"

With a smile he sat down beside me. "It's free."

Adel is a Palestinian Christian whose family has lived in Bethlehem for over 500 years. He is well-educated and traveled, and is the proud father of four children who have followed in his steps. While many of his family have left over the years in hopes of a less complicated life, Adel and his family are committed to the land and their home.

Our conversation came to a holt as Adel's phone rang. When he returned he informed me, "My friends are coming over now for coffee in the garden. Come, I want to show you."

Soon after, Adel swung shut his shop front; it was myself and three old men walking around the back of his house, to his prized garden. He showed me tree after tree, slowly picking samples off of each to taste: prunes, special olive-sized apples, almonds, and grapes. We sat in mismatched chairs around a dried-up stone fountain in the shade under an overhead trellis of grape vines.

As we sipped our second cup of Turkish coffee, Adnan, a professor of history at Bethlehem University, shared with me that he had traveled the world for his undergrad, masters, and PhD, but that he hasn't been into Jerusalem, the Holy City, a thirty-minute trip, in ten years. Every permit he has applied for, even for just one day- denied. The average Palestinian has access to less then twenty percent of a country that was without walls, check points, and the multitudes of armed guards just 65 years ago. Adnan looked at me, and not with eyes and a voice of anger, but with aged frustration and said, "You've heard that the West Bank is a prison?" I shook my head, yes.

"It is not a prison. It is a zoo. We are nothing but trapped animals for all the world to see as the multitudes pass through."

It was hard for me to understand how Adel, Adnan, and Joseph could be so kind to me. I was a tourist, one of the three million that pass through all the places they are denied access. I was also an American, a citizen of the nation that gives Israel most of its money and power. But in that moment I was their guest. Similar to Daoud, these three men are choosing to live a different way. And I would have spent the rest of the day with those old guys if I could have, but we were leaving for Bethany to return to the House of Hope.

Milad and Minar started the House of Hope because they wanted to do something to break the cycle of violence that had long penetrated the young people of their city. They had a humble start using their own house, but now they have grown into a building with a staff. Their mission is to provide a safe place for the children and young adults of Bethany to come for cultural and educational programs, in order to provide opportunities for a more hopeful future under occupation. House of Hope offers music, art, drama, dance, tutoring, and vocational training. But more than that, their staff of young adults, Christian and Muslim, mentor and build meaningful, consistent relationships with the hundreds of kids that are part of the program.

We were coming in to run a full day of activities for over one hundred elementary-age children. We divided ourselves up and then broke them into big groups that rotated activities throughout the day. One group worked on skits and another played a variety of games using balloons. There was a singing group that sang all sorts of songs. They sang Father Abraham. "Father Abraham had many sons. I am one of them, and so are you. So, let's all praise the Lord." There is not a more perfect song for Muslims and Christians to sing together as they try to build small bridges between cultures and religions.

John and I led soccer on the patio. The large patio was covered by a huge blue tarp to create shade. I was determined to learn every kid's name. This was not an easy task with a hundred Arabic names like Fatma, Omar, Abed, Yasmin, Coream, and Munsa. We broke them into lines and started with passing drills and headers. Before I'd toss the ball at their little heads I had them shout out their name. I'd say it back, they'd correct my pronunciation, I'd toss them the ball, they'd try to head it back, and then they'd run to the back of the line. We did it so many times that eventually I knew each little kid. For the rest of our time, we broke into two teams and scrimmaged. Soccer is a universal language. At the end of the day before these beautiful children piled out the gate to run back to their homes, there were many lingering hugs and even some tears. These are the children who will dictate the future of the conflict.

If there was any day that a shower was in order, it was this one. My already not-so-clean shirt had been drenched in sweat and air dried multiple times through out the day. But there were no showers that night because we would be spending the night sleeping on the floor of a couple of the classrooms in the House of Hope. Before we packed it in for a sticky night, Milad and Minar invited us to come to their house for a drink. Our four girls sat inside with Minar and she shared with us the story of how she met Milad and showed us their wedding album. She opened up to us and shared many things from the joys of marriage, to the challenges of occupation, to her hopes and dreams for the future. The guys sat outside, smoked, and drank vodka around a fire. This is what my friend Todd wrote about their time.

"The atmosphere shifted to a more serious tone as Milad asked our American guys to share their reflections of our time in the West Bank and with the House of Hope. Honored that they would ask, each person shared of their new-found understanding of the hospitality, occupation, Palestinians, Muslims, and the interfaith community displayed so beautifully throughout the children, staff, and volunteers at The House of Hope. After we shared, we asked the same question of our new Palestinian friends. We were overwhelmingly blessed by the transparency and openness that they all shared with. Stories of hardship, oppression, and hope rose to the surface of conversation, some of which had never been told before. Overwhelmingly, many of the reflections and responses went much like this, "Please tell of the beauty and humanity that you have found here. What you see on the news is not the whole story or even a proper snapshot of the people of Palestine. We have been blessed to meet you

*and have learned that there is a difference between "America"
and "Americans," but please don't forget us or our stories. Tell
the people back home what you have seen and heard."*

*Throughout this amazingly heartfelt time of sharing, I had to
continually remind myself that it was real. In a strange way, this
time was so powerful and beautiful that I found myself
overwhelmed, not knowing how to receive and process all that
was happening. Yes, I am in Bethany. Yes, I am sitting in a
circle sharing life and dreams with Palestinians, Muslims,
Christians, and Americans. And yes, this is all taking place in
the midst of occupation less then a half block from the
separation wall."*

day nine, ten, and eleven

In the morning, we left our friends at the House of Hope for Galilee. The Galilee is far removed from the conflict. The area is lush and beautiful and centers around a great lake called the Sea of Galilee. We were going there to decompress before we boarded a plane to return to the United States.

It was majestic and beautiful, but it was still crazy hot. It's the kind of heat you wade through. It tricks your eyes into seeing ripples and waves rise from the asphalt. It sucks all the moisture out of your mouth and burns the top of your ears. Despite the soaring temperatures, there was something special and refreshing about this place. The Sea of Galilee was the first thing that looked as I had imagined it in Sunday school. Everything else had been built into ridiculous-sized shrines flooded with tourists. But this lake was still a lake. We took a break from the steady flow of the falafel and hummus we'd had for three straight days and treated ourselves to burgers and lattes.

I liked this place.

On our second day in Galilee, we drove to Capernaum. This is the small fishing village on the lakeshore where Jesus lived in the beginning of his ministry after leaving Nazareth. He collected his first disciples, Peter, Andrew, James and John from here. They dropped their fishing nets and left all that they had to follow him. I sat in the ruins of the synagogue where Jesus taught and healed disease and sickness among the people. From the synagogue you could see the ruins of the foundations of the homes that made up the neighborhoods of Capernaum. From where I sat I wondered which house Jesus visited when the friends of a paralyzed man climbed up on the roof and dug a hole to lower their friend down, hoping that Jesus would heal him.

We walked out to the water. The shore was lined with large rocks. One of our own, Sarah, asked if she could be baptized. We all stood on the rocks as she, her husband, and Jer, climbed down into the water. With gentle waves breaking around them they got their footing and we watched with anticipation. Jer and Jeff dipped her back into the sea and for a second she disappeared, and when she came back up to the surface she had joy written all across her face. We cheered, clapped, hollered and then jumped in to join them. It was glorious. There is nothing so special as being baptized in the same water Jesus walked across. As we walked back to the entrance by the ruins of the synagogue in our sopping wet clothes, a monk reprimanded us for getting in the water. We didn't care.

Issa drove us to the Mount of Beatitudes to visit the shoreside hill where Jesus gave the famous Sermon on the Mount, found in the fifth chapter of Matthew. "Blessed are the poor in spirit, for theirs is the kingdom of heaven. Blessed are those who mourn, for they will be comforted. Blessed are the meek, for they will inherit the the earth... Blessed are the peacemakers, for they will be called sons of God."

Again this place was not how I had imagined it. It was a manicured tourist destination with gift shops and rose bushes. We tried to sit on the grass facing the sea to read through Jesus' most central teaching in the very spot where he taught it. Within moments of sitting down, a nun standing far off with a microphone yelled at us over a loud speaker that echoed for all to hear, "You cannot sit there! Off the grass! Off the grass!" This time we cared.

When we got back to the hotel, we changed into our swimsuits to take full advantage of swimming in the Galilee. This time we went down to a sandy shore, and in the distance there was an outcropping of rocks that we saw some boys jumping off the night before. JD had a ziplock bag, so we all gave him our passports to keep them safe in the pocket of his board shorts. I made the long swim out to the rocks. The water was like none I had swam in before. It was an opaque, vibrant green. With as much air as my lungs could hold, I swam straight down, and all I could see was my hands and green. I was struck by the silence and the peace that I found under that water. It felt like the first time in over a week that everything stopped and was truly quiet. When I made it to the rocks, they weren't actually rocks, but a bundle of metal drums hot enough to cook an egg. After splashing water to cool them off, lacking any grace, I pulled myself up with a chain, a bolt, and a grunt. Jockeying for balance on the now heavily-leaning drums, I stood up straight and proud. I felt an intense satisfaction standing in the middle of the Galilee. In that moment it was impossible to ignore the importance of all that had happened. And soon it would be my time to share all that I had seen and heard. I was excited to be part of taking the energy behind my frustration and channel it into something positive. If I knew how to do a flip I would have. Instead, I jumped in and once back on the shore, JD pulled out the zip-lock bag from his pocket, full of water. Our passports were fully submerged.

That evening in the hotel's lobby we spent a lot of time as a group discussing and downloading about the experience of our last ten days. We each tried to form an answer to the question we knew many would ask once we returned home, "How was your trip?" Seems simple like a simple question, but it is a complicated and confusing answer. We spread out and spent an hour writing an answer to that question, and then we came back into our circle to share our response. What I wrote was, "It was complicated. I found out that Israel/Palestine is full of human beings. Two groups that are more the same than they are different. They are both traumatized by hate, and they are both willing to die before they give up their land. The hope lies in the few who haven't been blinded by hate, and see the people on the other side of the wall as human beings." When it came to my turn to share, what I actually said to my friends that night was, "Every day just continually f-ed with my head and my heart. I felt like it was a constant tug-of-war between two groups of people who were more the same than they were different. It wasn't until the day that I met someone who truly understood what peace is that I was even able to stand up on something that made sense. And it was like a big toaster oven over there, really hot."

On our way to the airport, we stopped for dinner in westernized Tel-Aviv at a restaurant that looked out onto the Mediterranean. The sunset over the sea was breathtaking. It was hard to believe that the place we were eating dinner was part of the same country we had just come from. Once at Ben Gurion's airport we made it through the intense airport security, despite damp passports, and buckled up for a very long journey home.

After a few long flights and several missed nights of sleep, during a layover in Turkey, I was sound asleep sprawled out on an airport bench when I was abruptly woken up by two little rascal children jumping up and down on the end of my bench. With bed head and still groggy the man next to me asked where I had come from. He was with his wife and daughter returning home to England after a trip to Iran to visit extended family. When I told him I had come from Israel/Palestine he leaned in, "May I ask why you were there?" When I told him about the purpose of our trip, having to work extra hard to make complete sentences, he was very intrigued. "So, what did you find out?" After telling him bits and pieces of what we saw and experienced he interrupted me, "But whose side are you on?" When I said we went there in order to hear the stories of both, and to stand with those pursuing peace, he was instantly frustrated with my answer. "That is propaganda, just meaningless words. Tell the truth! Whose side are you on?" He then began to tell me about all that my country has done to Iran, and how horrible America is. Quite a few times I tried to diffuse his anger, but eventually I had to walk away.

It was then that I realized that it wasn't going to be easy to share what we had learned and experienced. And many people were not going to agree with me. But, I knew my job was to share the stories, whether they were accepted or not. People are bound to disagree, but if it forces anyone to ask questions of what they had once blindly accepted to be true, then we have succeeded. And the people who courageously shared their lives with us in Israel and the West Bank are valued.

Unfortunately, I had to work the next morning after our two marathon days of air travel. Jet-lagged and dragging my feet, I drove to work, got my swimsuit on, and slipped into the swimming pool where I teach private swim lessons. My first lesson was late, leaving me alone in the pool backing onto Northern California's beautiful open spaces. Taken by my emotions, I began to cry. It was the overwhelming peace I felt in the quiet and the calm of the water that did it. I have never been very patriotic, but standing waist-deep in that pool, I was thankful for my freedom in a way I had never been before. I was home safe, free from the constant tension and the hate, but they are still there.

We no longer have the luxury of being ignorant, and with that comes responsibility. What we choose to do with that responsibility is up to us.

Liel refuses to blindly obey the government in which he was born into. Husam refuses to stop chasing down his passions despite obstacles and barriers. Eliyahu refuses to embrace a one-sided story, and anything short of peace. Tsipi refuses to forget by commemorating the past and building for the future. Adeeb refuses to throw the rocks his peers and culture expect of him. Daoud refuses to be enemies with those who persecute him. Adel refuses to see people as anything other than his guests. Milad and Manar refuse to let the cycle of violence continue in their children.

I refuse to be ignorant and apathetic. For some reason, beyond my understanding, we were born here into freedom and endless opportunity, and the people of Israel and the West Bank, and many other countries of the world were born into places racked with conflict and oppression. If the situation was switched, and we were there and they were here, I can only imagine that we would long for someone to care about our suffering.

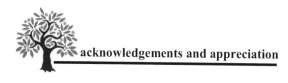

acknowledgements and appreciation

This project was a collaboration of love by my friends and community. Many thanks are warranted.

Thanks to Jer and Jon and the Global Immersion Project for opening my eyes to the people of Israel/Palestine, and for providing a unique experience to inspire and fuel the writing.

Thanks to our brave story-tellers: Issa, Liel, Hussam, Tsipi, Eliyahu, Adeeb, Rhebi, Nidal, Walid, Daoud, Adel, Adnan, Milad, Minar, and the House of Hope staff.

Thanks to those who helped with and attended the fundraiser "Alongside a Lion" readings in California and Florida.

Thanks to those who generously gave in order to fund my trip and this project: Mike and Robyn Shapiro, David and Janyce Hoyt, Tim and Lois Halls, Christine Hintzoglou, Les and Maralyn Comee, Kathy Andree-Rissel, Gail Jones, Stan and Carol Hasegawa, Marsi and John Girardi, Kerry and Charlene O'Brien, Kara and Paul Lynch, Tyler Hargen, Tony Collins, Mark Brosamer, Mike and Claire Mozley, Beverly Hubric, Amy Dyson, Susan McCormack, Jerry McCormack, Michael and Francesca MacDonald, Samantha Bizet, Jenna Wimmer, Kelly Knox, Aaron Ankrum, Donna Frasier, Krissy Holland, Julie and Mark Stover.

Thanks to those that entered into this experience alongside me: Jer Swigart, JD and Kristen Kessler, Sarah and Jeff Rutledge, John Hamilton, Jon Hukins, Todd and Jenna Rubie, Derek Rice, Carli Aanderud, Nick Foran, and Geoff Mayfield.

Thanks to Sarah Rutledge, Keiko Arimitsu, Susan McCormack, Beverly Hubric, and Mark Brosamer for first, second, and third-round edits. Thanks to John Hamilton and Matt Jenson for your photography. Thanks to Josh Hockom for entering into my formatting nightmare. And thanks to Robert Mitchell and M.L. for your patience and your incredible design work.

More about...
The Global Immersion Project

The mission of the The Global Immersion Project is to cultivate everyday peacemakers through immersion in global conflict. We are a global organization that believes in the just impact, locally and globally, that North Americans can make if we learn to live in the posture of a learner with God, ourselves, each other, and those who inhabit our global village.

Our learning communities are open to various genres of difference-makers (marketplace leaders, educators, artists, local church leaders, non-profit entrepreneurs, etc.) that commit to a four month course that culminates in a 12 day experience on the ground in Israel and the West Bank, Palestine.

Our cultivation will take place in three phases: (1) understanding; (2) exposure; and (3) integration. The understanding phase begins as our learning community reads literature, watches documentaries, immerses in the Scriptures, meets local Israelis and Palestinians, and processes what we're learning. The exposure phase occurs on the ground in the Holy Land as we share time with new friends (Israeli and Palestinian) who have lived and will share diverse narratives of life in conflict. This middle phase involves shared tables, friendship-making, and historical and contemporary storytelling in the places where history (ancient and more recent) has been and where contemporary life is being lived out. We will find ourselves in the middle of injustice, pain, collective suffering, celebration, hope, and reconciliation.

The integration phase begins during our last two days of the experience. Together, we will process and learn from our journey as a whole while gaining the necessary resources to live as difference-makers within our North American contexts. Understanding that our work begins upon our return, it is in this third phase that we will begin formalizing answers to the "What now?" question and exploring myriad ways of living as just influencers here. The hope is that we would continue to develop into people who tangibly live, love, and lead like Jesus.

Find out more at http://theglobalimmersionproject.com/

 **resources**

Books

Adwan, Bar-On, and Naven. Side by Side. New York: The New Press, 2012.

Andrew, Brother. Light Force. Grand Rapids, MI: Revell, 2004

Ashouri, Sami. Is the Qur'an God's Word? Beltsville, MD: Amna Publictions, 2005.

Ben-Gurion, David. Israel: Years of Challenge. New York: Massadah-P.E.C. Press, 1963.

Chacour, Eli. Blood Brothers. Grand Rapids, MI: Chosen Books, 2003.

Joffe, Lawrence. Jewish People. Leicestershire, ENG: Anness Publishing, 2012.

Learner, Rabbi Michael. Embracing Israel/Palestine. Berkeley, CA: Tikkun Books, 2012.

Sizer, Steven. Christian Zionism. Downers Grove, IL: Intervarsity Press, 2004.

Thomas, Amelia. Lonely Planet: Israel and the Palestinian Territories. China: Lonely Planet, 2010.

Volf, Miroslav. Allah. New York: Harper One, 2011.

Websites

United Nations Statistic Division- unstats.un.org

Statistics- www.ifamericansknew.com

History Timelines- www.wikepedia.com

Israel Ministry of Foreign Affairs- www.mfa.gov

Palestinian National Authority- worldstatesmen.org

Tent of Nations- www.tentofnations.org

The House of Hope- www.hohbethlehem.org

The Global Immersion Project- www.theglobalimmersionproject.com

Current News- www.bbc.news.com

Documentaries and Film

Bolado, C. (Director). (2001). Promises. (Documentary). United
    States: Israel.

Cedar, J. (Director). (2000). Time of Favor. (Motion Picture). Israel.

Daum, M. (Director). (2004). Hiding and Seeking: Faith and Tolerance
    after the Holocaust. (Documentary). Israel.

David, K. (Actor). (2003). Empires: The Kingdom of David.
    (Documentary). United States.

Gilbert, M. (Actor). (1997). Israel: Birth of a Nation. (Documentary).
    United States.

Gitai, A. (Director). (2002). Ketma. (Motion Picture). Israel.

Goldberg, A. (Director). (2009). The Jewish People: A Story of
    Survival. (Documentary). United States.

Kiley, R. (Actor). (2005). Mysteries of the Bible: Abraham, One man,
    One God. (Documentary). United States.

National Geographic (Producer). (2011). Secrets of Jerusalem's Holiest
    Sites. (Documentary). United States.

Quigley, A. (Director). (2005). Diameter of the Bomb. (Documentary).
    Hungary.

Riklis, E. (Director). (2008). Lemon Tree. (Motion Picture). Israel:
    Germany: France.

Sinnocrat, N. (Director). (2006). Palestinian Blues. (Documentary).
    United States.

Wasson, J. (Director). (2010). Surviving Hitler. (Documentary). United
    States.

Made in the USA
San Bernardino, CA
06 November 2013